D1192218

MY BROTHER DENNIS

DENNIS BENSON

MY BROTHER DENNIS

DENNIS BENSON

WORD BOOKS, PUBLISHER   •   WACO, TEXAS

My Brother Dennis

Copyright © 1975 by Dennis C. Benson. All rights reserved. No part of this book may be reproduced in any form, except for brief quotations in reviews, without the written permission of the publisher.

Printed in the United States of America

Library of Congress card catalog number: 75—10092

Contents

1 Getting Ready   7

2 Getting Set 14

3 Going 17

4 A Long News Break 86

5 The Second Hour 104

6 Coming Down 183

7 Closing Credits 186

1 Getting Ready

It happened when I was sixteen years old. My family was understanding and did what they could to help me through the painful process of becoming. There weren't any unusual problems at school. My part-time job at the shoe store was even going well. Yet, it suddenly became vital that I find a *significant other*. Someone whom I could confide in and share with on a deep level of trust. Someone who would see me as a person of worth. This someone just happened to be an adult, Jess Waller.

Jess's attributes were common to every person who is a significant other. He listened well. I could drop by and talk about anything. He wasn't shocked or bored. I can't remember a thing he ever told me. It's not clear if he was wise or even gave advice.

Jess's second attribute was his accessibility at a key point in my development. I was struggling to make some sense out of my life and looking for the future. Many of my current actions were resulting in blind alleys. At this junction of past and future I needed someone outside of my close family setting who would give me perspective. I found Jess because I needed him. Jess happened to be a church worker. However, he or she as a significant other could have been a teacher, town drunk, coach, widow, uncle, or pop star.

Jess also was a very warm and responsive person. This attribute is also a common trait in significant others. He seemed to be able to take all of my feelings and person-hood in. I felt accepted and I was willing to risk being fully human in his presence. Most of my other interactions at the time would not permit this kind of honesty. I felt judged and evaluated at school, home, and by my peers. Jess projected a sense of care and acceptance that per-mitted me to externalize what was budding inside.

The person playing this transitional role in the life of those who are maturing or facing a crisis has a bigger-than-life status based on openness rather than outstanding abilities. I could easily see through the world of my adult friend. It was always easy for me to delineate his faults and limitations. The important role he played at that point in my life was grounded in his human attributes—strengths *and* weaknesses.

There have been many persons who have listened and given love to Dennis in the years since I sat in the Waller living room drinking Pepsi and moaning about the loves lost, the future clouded, or the past mourned. So many have given so much of themselves to me that, in turn, I have found myself becoming a significant other in the lives of other people.

Along the way I have had special experiences which give my Christian motivation to be a friend more depth than might be the case. As a hospital chaplain, I dis-covered the strength and power to be a significant other as persons were enabled to be strong and faithful in very tragic circumstances. There have been moments when three or four of us sat and cried together over the death of a child. Yet, someone would emerge as an enabler for the rest of us to draw upon the hope and peace that is possible in every situation. More often than not, in the role of the significant other I would be the one to receive ministry from grieving parents.

My days of serving as a college chaplain quickened me to discover the resources and gifts of the young. We were together and much happened.

I became a significant other. Yet, one night the tables became turned. I had just been fired and my critics tried to disgrace me for working with the black students on campus. Dave Smith, a beautiful black athlete who stood with me in our fight for equal housing, suddenly appeared in our living room. We were outcasts in the small Pennsylvania town. Our faculty friends had left campus for the summer and we were waiting in hopes of finding another job. The prospects were bleak. Dave spent an evening with Marilyn and me. Afterwards he told a mutual friend that he had to show up because "Dennis needed someone."

This book deals with my most immediate experience of being a significant person to others. The arena in which these encounters took place is most unusual. It didn't take place in a hospital waiting room, living room, college coffee house, or local bar. Most of the encounters occurred through the mail. No, it is really more complex than that. For three years I was host of a popular radio show on an ABC radio station in Pittsburgh, Pennsylvania, called *Rap Around*. The station asked me to do a phone call-in program which would win the imaginations of the audience listening to this top-forty outlet. I came on the air just after we had rocked and boogied for twelve hours.

I was not happy with the type of talk radio we had in our media market. One host would scream at the listeners and insult those who called. Another radio personality would agree with every opinion expressed by callers. I suspected that radio had the capacity to convey feelings.

Many disc jockeys had told me about the calls they got from listeners. Their stories suggested the pattern I had chartered in my theories of being a significant other. The fact that a person was known in the context of a listener's music gave him or her immediate significance. The role of music in struggling with feelings is most important. The sound environment means a great deal to the listener. (See a more complete discussion on this interaction in *The Now Generation*, John Knox Press.) The DJ is intimately involved in this electronic confessional.

Rap Around was an attempt to utilize radio to be significant to the feelings and development of others. I even tried to approach the "content" or "issue" exchanges from a feeling perspective. Soon a young woman shared her fear of being pregnant and having been deserted by her boyfriend. The pattern of having been cared for by others was impressed upon me as I tried to befriend this person with my feeling and voice. It was not a counseling situation. We were on the radio and I could not see her. It would probably fall under the category of a "pre-counseling" encounter. Yet, I was being a significant other to this person, reaching out at a moment of change, reflection, and crisis. Our broadcast conversation led to another private call and a referral for counseling. She actually went from a radio phone call to an in-person counseling situation!

Soon all our calls were of a personal nature. Everyone wanted to offer a problem or feeling. I would leave the two-hour experience totally exhausted. It is so hard to listen, to give, and share vibrations with others. Our phone lines would be full an hour before the show. I would often take calls for another two hours after we were off the air. Brother Patrick Carney, a Christian brother and math teacher in a local Roman Catholic high school, was the phone producer.

Then the mail started to come. Russell Martz, public affairs director at the station, arranged secretarial assistance so that I could dictate answers to all the letters. We started running fifty to one hundred letters a week during this early phase. That's what this book is about. I will share moments from the lives of other people. It is my hope that the quality and nature of our love exchange will emerge along the way. This is not an "Ann Landers" or "Dear Abby" book. I am not an answer kind of person in the role of being significant to others. I am simply a significant other who really cares. I was aware of the limitations placed on me in this clearly defined public situation.

The hundred or more people you will meet in this book are very dear to me. I have changed names, places, and even chronology to protect these good folk. You and I will experience the agony of wanting to know more, feel more, and do more for some we will meet. This is one of the prices to be paid when you are a significant other. You are not permitted a fluid intimacy or even friendship in which this kind of healing can take place. You are just a way station of human warmth along the road. Some stop and find a moment of shelter and hope before hitting the road and facing the storm of life once again. These folks will underscore the kind of humanity such encounters impress upon the significant other.

I am sharing a debriefing of my heart and mind as I reflect over one of the most important segments of my life. I hope that you will not judge me harshly when I do not appear wise enough, loving enough, or patient enough for a particular occasion. Perhaps you will discover some keys or clues for your own human giving from my mistakes.

It has been very hard going over the letters and tapes

11

of the shows from the past. Certain smells, sights, and sounds are recalled as I flash back to the hours in my study when I read these epistles for the first time and answered them. I fondly remember an evening when five-year-old Amy scribbled on small pieces of paper at the left hand side of my desk while I dictated. "I am writing letters to help people who are lonely and sad."

There are some folks who have brought tears to my eyes once again as their lives stir within me. I hope that emotionally I can get to the point of sharing certain people with you. Some of this is still very hard to feel all over again.

I offer my folk and our modest relationship in the hope that it may be of help in the ministry of being significant to the young and old around you. This low profile style of relationship may be the very glue which holds a community together. With your face-to-face environment, the chances for really giving and receiving personhood is even much stronger than the kind of relationship suggested here. However, the possibilities of in-depth relationship will elude you without the kind of sensitivities exercised in the significant other style of encounter. We must be emotionally hospitable before we can be a friend or lover.

As much as we know that nothing can substitute for a face-to-face encounter, the media of radio and the written word are powerful. We must utilize every opportunity to use the means at hand to exchange some of the attributes of personhood with another. There is much to be given by each of us to others. There is also much to be received from them. It is this transaction which can change the lives of those in your community and family. It is good to seek to be a significant other.

You are invited to participate in a meandering journal of the radio/epistle journey of one in quest of being a significant other. The flood of feelings, ideas, and people may defy the comfort of logic under the control of recall. May the benchmark of care overcome any frustration at what is coming. Enter the world of *Rap Around* and its quest to be a significant other—as caught in the emotion of retrospection.

2 Getting Set

I pushed the buzzer between the locked, swinging doors. Russ Nelson, the watchman, smiled and opened the special entrance for those coming into the building which housed KQV. Brother Pat was already getting set for the evening's show. He always came early. We would have many calls before we hit the air at 9:00 *P.M.* Little did I suspect the changes which would come in the course of two years together. Pat would find misunderstanding and even hostility from some people within his order because of his work with me on *Rap Around*. This would eventually lead to his departure from the city. However, this change of events would be for the future.

We rapped about the thrust of the show. My briefcase was filled with the letters of the past week. We left the cassette tapes of dictation for Suzie. She would pass them on to typists for transcription. If lucky, my folks would have answers to their letters within the week.

I am always excited as I enter the broadcast area. Studio B is poorly insulated. I can hear the sounds from the air studio coming through the floor. Jim Carnegie is pumping out the top forty sounds from Studio A. This room is also always cool. Summer and winter give us the same freezer-locker kind of physical experience. Yet, this kind of environment gives me the mental image that I am in a state of suspended animation. The sound of callers' voices become the only reality. It helps to open the curtains and let the sights of the business street and sidewalk flood this special environment where I will try to listen, feel, and share.

"I have a problem." Engineer John Yurek, smiles and waves from the master control area. He has to use the intercom system to talk with me. We are separated by a soundproof wall of glass. He is one of the more responsive engineers for the show. He checks out our phone-talk system well in advance of air time. We use a Band-Aid system which involves two tape machines and a roll of audio tape which stretches in an eight-foot loop. This gives us a six second delay.

I like the feeling of being behind this board. The rows of switches, pots (knobs), and slides (fancier knobs), give one a sense of oneness with the controls. The mike is suspended over the board. It is easy to work it close. I have to do this. My voice is bad. I want to be as intimate with the caller as the mike will permit. Our kind of communication calls for the voice quality of lovers. We can be as close and tender as lovers cuddling in bed, parent and child snuggling in a rocking chair, dying patient and chaplain holding hands at a hospital bedside, or priest and parishioner whispering in the confessional. We only have our voices to communicate our personhoods on *Rap Around*. We must make contact as a person so as not to fail. There is such a fine line between being with someone in spirit and mocking another's pain. Such thoughts bring a sweeping wave of uncertainty once again. The couple of hours before the show are always hard.

John is asking for a check of equipment. It is good sitting behind the board. The headset (earphones) feel good.

There is a sense of being able to hear the whole environment more completely. "1-2-3-4-5-6-7." It is immediately clear that I am talking too fast. Even the testing of our system warns me to slow down and feel with my voice and spirit. Everything checks out.

Pat and I both keep a log of the calls taken on the air. This is needed for our Public Affairs records. It also helps me keep a bearing on where all the rap is going. It is hard to keep papers from rattling. Yet, there are usually fifteen or more letters before me as reference points or content for the show.

Mark Schaffer has now started his five-minute newscast. Race horses at the gate, and people about to face the electric chair must share in this feeling. My throat has become tight. A swallow of Coke helps a bit. The mike button is pushed. John will turn me on from master control. This will eliminate the loud click which results from turning the instrument on from Studio B. Jim throws a cue from Studio A. He has to run the opening cartridge from outside our room to get us on the six-second delay. This protects us from the possibility of someone using names to libel someone or perhaps saying something which the FCC wouldn't permit us to air.

I can't hear the opening in my headset. Yet, I know what the audience is hearing. The opening drum solo from my theme can be heard. I love this portion of the Rolling Stones' masterpiece, "Sympathy for the Devil." Bob Wilson must now be giving his taped introduction to our special kind of two hours. Now is the chance to bring it altogether and try to become a community. Who is out there? What will we talk about? Can we match vibes in such a way that communication of persons will happen? It is time to go about it.

16

3 Going

9:00—Theme and Introduction (opening cartridge)

"Welcome, brothers and sisters, to our *Rap Around* community. We have a chance to share who we are and where we are. We are not here to answer problems or dispense wisdom. However, we have the hunch that it is possible to really be with each other. It helps honestly to struggle with how we feel with someone who cares. I care about you. We get letters from all kinds of people. People of all ages. There are people in our community tonight who are lonely, sick, bored, or just confused. We get letters from lesbians, homosexuals, the alienated, and the confused. We do care about you. There is nothing which we cannot endure and overcome if we draw upon the kind of help that is available in our community. I have friends who won't rip you off. Folk who help make the kinds of decisions *you* must make about your life. Our number is 333-9190. Our good brother, Pat, will help you get set for being on the air. When you talk with him you are already related to *Rap Around*. He is a good brother."

It is hard to get into the show. It always seems that I am putting words on top of each other. There is nothing written before me. I have never been able to read material and have it sound like it is real. The words are just coming from somewhere inside.

Dear Dennis Benson,
A few weeks ago I turned on my radio in hopes of some good music. Instead I heard you and the introduction of some freaky talk show. As I heard the native drums sound, or rather, beat, I thought, "Oh, no. Another damn talk show." I am used to those issue talk shows. The same boring positions stated over and over. As you started, though, I became interested. "Is this guy for real?" I thought it was a put-on, but I was surprised. You are sincere. . . .

9:02—Adult woman called to question the character of Dennis. Who is Dennis Benson? What is he trying to do? What kind of background does he have? What does he look like?

Dear Dennis,
I've wanted to write you for such a long time . . . You really have a great voice. Sexy but sincere. What do you look like? Will ya send me a pic?

We have sent out 200 pictures. It was a mistake. The mail in response to the pictures has been strange. It seems that people want to picture their significant other in their own mind.

Den,
I received your photo as I requested and your letter. Thank you. My only objection to the photo is that it's too formal. It reminds me of a child that's been scrubbed squeaky clean, hair combed in place and told to stand in a corner and don't dare to get dirty. . . .

Dennis Benson,

I still can't accept how you look. I pictured you as being tall and blond. You sound like the kind of person who would wear sweaters and tennis shoes. I can't get over it. . . .

Denny,

Thanks for the picture you sent. I didn't think that you would have a beard and long hair. I don't know why I figured you looked this way. Guess my imagination pictures you in a different way. . . .

Dennis,

Your pic makes you old. I thought you were younger. You sound young. I mean, you sound like you are just out of high school. . . .

Dear Dennis,

I can't believe the picture you sent me. I thought that you were black. You sound like a black man. It doesn't make any difference. It is just strange how different you look. . . .

Perhaps one of the most important links which brings our community together is our mutual imaginary visual projections. I also draw pictures in my mind when I listen to the *Rap Around* folk. It makes our conversation easier. When we reach out and touch another in the quest for help, it might be particularly useful if we don't know how he or she looks. We can project any comforting image we need. Our kind of communication hangs together by threads. We need everything we can use to be human to each other under these circumstances. Next time I will remain without a face for these folk. Let them trust one whom they cannot see.

Dear Dennis Benson,

I received your letter this week. Thank you for your picture. You are a handsome young man. It helps me to know what you look like. I am the lady that is 72. I wrote to you before. I like rock and roll, but not all. Some come out with the words plainer than others. Keep up the good work. I listen all the time you are on. . . .

We had a short conversation. I hope that the lady wasn't put off because we didn't go into the questions from a biographical angle. Why the probes about trust? Was she trying to discern if we really cared about the kids? Was she pushing me to see if I would admit that I am a Presbyterian clergyman? I didn't mention it. Was this a dodge? Does this reflect my fear of being rejected by the kids if they found out?

Dear Dennis Benson,
First, I would like to compliment you on the excellent job you are doing with your show. I praise the Lord for your special and very effective ministry. I also want you to know that I knew you are a minister even before you told us. . . .

9:05—A boy called and asked what Dennis C. Benson thought about obscene calls. This boy's voice seems familiar.

He must be the one who has called for the past few weeks and called me names. One week he proclaimed that I was a "fag." He would just hang up and not let me reply. We let the comments go on the air. It will be important that I handle this one carefully. It is not the fear of obscenities on the air that worries. These can always be cut off the air with one push of my "panic fill" box.

His voice is very tight. A note from Pat suggests that he had a hard time in the initial rap with him. Is he testing me? Is this an opportunity to enact the kind of love and care we are suggesting on *Rap Around?*

20

"I can't understand why people get so upset over people who make obscene calls. Well . . . it might shock or offend them. But . . . I suspect that people who make such calls are really trying to reach out and communicate. It is just that they are uptight. It seems best that we just show such folk that we love them. Everyone needs love.

"Ya, I need love too."

I couldn't know at the time that this would be the last of such calls to our program. Perhaps he felt some of the acceptance that we were trying to enact. It is our naive assumption that when people are treated with respect, they will respect in return.

9:07—An eighteen-year-old girl calls and talks about loneliness. She just hides in her mother's apartment. She has no friends and longs to talk with others.

The letter is messy. Ann has struck out many words. The styles of handwriting seem to change in the course of the letter.

Mr. Benson,
Well, I don't know how to start. Really I shouldn't even be writing (in fact I *am very drunk* now just so I could write this letter) for I am *very shy* and I can not talk to anyone about problems (I don't know why) even my close friends but they talk about there's. Don't think I am an alcoholic because I am now drunk so I could write this, but I do drink at least 3 times aweek (alot), because I am *not* an alcoholic (really).
Well here goes: boys do not like me. I am 19 and no one knows but I have not had a date all my life. I am sort of ugly and I don't have a personality to get them either. I go to parties and

21

stuff to meet boys but all they want is sex something. The only guy that *seems* to really like me is a black man who is really nice. My parents would kill me. . . . I have 2 jobs all summer and got laid off on one and fired from the other. I never went out with this black guy, but he took me home when ever he saw me drunk. I *think* I like him a awful lot.

You know it feels good just to wright this junk down. For the first night in about three years I am not spending an evening at home crying.

Forget that I am now crying!

I feel very lonely right now and I wished I would stop crying. If you are still reading this stupid letter, I am very surprised and you must think I'm crazy.

I will not go into my other silly problems because if you are still reading this I don't want you to have to go on. Thank-you it feels funny to for once express myself. I am going to mail this now while I am drunk or else I would never mail it. . . .

Dear Ann,

Your letter hit me in a very hard way. I feel very strongly about what you are going through. It's so very hard to be lonely and out of touch. I can imagine the agony and pain you must be experiencing. It must have been very hard for you to write that letter. Yet, your letter revealed so much about you as a person. You have a will and desire to love and reach out and touch people. This is wonderful.

Fight your despair. I think that there are ways by which you could get into touch with people. I strongly suggest that you find somebody with whom you can talk about your problems. You'll be amazed how it clears up things to have someone else enable you to see what's going on and give you some options concerning your present life. Why don't you call me during the day? My number is . . . .

The important thing about your letter was that you attempted to reach out and share your loneliness with someone else. This indicates that you can reach out and that you can change the direction of your life. This is a sign of hope and possibility for you. I care about you. Please call me. . . .

Dear Mr. Benson,

I don't remember exactly what I wrote to you about some of my problems, but it was all true. I hope that this letter would get lost in the mail, but it didn't. When I got your letter back, it took me three days before I opened it. I was so embarassed by all those things I told you.

I haven't called you. I couldn't even do that. I'm too scared and don't know what to say. I can't talk to anyone. I guess that's why I love to drink.

You also said that my letter indicated that I can reach out and change the direction of my life, but I said things I said when I was drunk and I can't say those things when I am sober.

Please tell me how I can open up to other people or should I just be myself and keep quiet as I have for the 19 years of my life? I am sorry I bothered you with my stupid letter, but somehow it makes me feel a little better. . . .

Dear Mr. Benson,

Here I am again writing to you. . . . I felt so selfish taking time you could be helping someone that matters and someone who can be helped. Thank you very much, you have *really* helped me from doing something desperate. *Please* if you are busy, don't bother to answer this. . . .

We finally did talk. We were never able to get her to a counseling service. Our conversations were quiet. She would sometimes not talk for two or three minutes. It was just a time of presence and not verbal communication.

Finally, her letters stopped coming. Is she in community now? Does she still drink and cry? Why doesn't she write? Is she listening tonight? Will my conversation with this lonely girl support Ann?

9:12—A high school girl calls about her boyfriend. She loves a guy, but he doesn't seem to like her.

This is the kind of problem that is rejected by most adults. So often people can't identify with another person's unsuccessful quest to find another person. This is especially true when the person is a teenager.

On *Rap Around*, we are going to care about everyone! If you hurt, it is important. It is not the objective degree of the problem's seriousness which is important. The emotional context of the concern gives it value to us. It is so difficult for every person to feel with others' non-fatal crises.

> Dear Den,
> I listened to your show last week. I like it, but there are so many dopy people calling in. They have such silly problems. Who cares about a lost boyfriend or "how can I get him to notice me?" You should cut them off.
> Now I have a real problem. . . .

> Dennis,
> . . . Also, I dig the way you take people at face value. Always assume they tell the truth and they will tell it more and more.
> A 14 year old girl called and said she was in love with a guy. She's probably been filled with, "You don't know what love is," or, "You are too young to be in love." You didn't say that. It's great. She needed someone to believe her and you did it. Her love is just as real to her as anyone else's is to them. Love is a personal thing. To be shared, yes, but not defined.

24

George has expressed it so well! It is my hunch that the handling of "minor" or the less sensational problems provides the foundation for gaining the confidence of those with more serious situations.

> Dear Brother Dennis,
>   I have listened to *Rap Around* for the whole time it has been on the air. If you listen to those dumb problems of kids, I know that you will understand mine.
>   A couple years ago my husband got drunk and killed our baby by accident. He buried Danny in the cemetery himself. The police found out and put him in jail.
>   I lost custody of my other children. I had a little nervous breakdown. I haven't heard from my husband since he went to jail. I love my man and my children. How can I get them back?

I take another swig of Coke. The noise of the liquid hissing in the bottle comes through the mike. The headset really makes you aware of the noise environment. It is time to identify the show and restate our concept of community and sharing. It is important that we define feelings as being acceptable as a level of communication.

9:16—A lady calls in regard to the previous call concerning the lonely woman. She wants to help her. Could we put them in touch with each other?

> Dennis,
>   I am blind and can't talk well. That girl who had no friends, I will be happy to be friends. Give her my address and let her write if she wants to.
>   I want to start a correspondence. Let her decide if she wants a correspondence.

The lady on the phone and John's postcard reflect the amazing side effects of publicly rehearsing the process of being significant to others. Those who experience care often want to care in return. The growth of volunteerism reflects the uncaptured imaginations for service which exist in the population. Too many people are trapped into venting their personhood toward animals when humans are emotionally bleeding. My young daughters would be critical of this comparison. However, the weekly input from human loneliness through the *Rap Around* community continually shocked my perspective. The world of advertising plays to this hunger for acceptance and love.

It is time for more liquid down the throat. I have not talked much on tonight's show. Only when we listened to the weekly air check tapes of the show was it realized why so much throat lubrication is needed. In the course of the conversations, I continually make a slight noise indicating affirmation. This doesn't mean that I necessarily agreed with the viewpoint of the caller. This collection of non-articulate sounds is a means of affirming the caller's right to share feelings. It is interesting to listen to my moans and slight sighs which follow a person's unburdening of a very important concern. This audio process is somewhat like the body language we use in situations where we are in physical range of others. It is also an extension of the facial expressions which are vital to close communication in caring situations. The impact of sound's power is over-whelming. We so often work only within a very narrow band of audio communication.

Pat and I have had to fight our empathy at some points. It is easy to get "down" or depressed in our link with the audience. The others who are part of the caring web have only sound to sustain their impression of what is happening in this onrush to communication probes.

Dear Dennis,
    Hi. I want to thank you for answering my letter,

not long ago. I really appreciated it. I just got finished listening to your program tonight—and maybe I'm just imagining things—but to me, you sounded rather low. You just didn't seem like your usual self—I don't know. I probably was just imagining it. But it just seemed that way to me. But I hope it wasn't true. . . . Anyway, I have written you a poem of hope to cheer you up. It is enclosed with my letter. . . .

Judy may have been projecting. However, it is amazing how sensitive consistent listeners can be to the person at the other end of the relationship. Much perspective is needed to fight the temptation to flee into despair. The *Rap Around* kind of exposure to people in an electronic web, who do not touch institutions or helping agencies, can be frightening.

Dear Dennis,
    I would like to say I enjoy your radio program very much. I'm writing to you because I have a *really big* problem.
    I am a guy and I'm 24 years old and I can't get a girlfriend because I'm very shy around girls. I have a *terrible* time talking to girls. *Please* believe everything I tell you in this letter. *Please* I wouldn't be writing to you if I have or could get a girlfriend. *Please* believe this letter. I must have some kind of mental illness. I feel so *terribly* lonely right now that it would probably be hard for you to imagine. I've been *lonely* all my life.
    All that I really want out of this world is a girl to love. I want to find a girl who will love me just as much as I love her. I want *true* love. I guess this is a terrible thing to say but I've always dreamed of falling in love with a girl who was at least fairly nice looking. I don't want to hurt anyone in this whole world. I just want to love and be loved. I know what real love is, love

is trying your *best* to keep the other person happy. Love is an *everyday* thing. To me love isn't just sex. Love is being a real friend. I want to be loved for myself and treated like a *man*. Love is *give* and *take*. I want someone I can tell my problems to.

My past isn't perfect as far as girls go. When I was in the Navy, I went to many prostitutes and ended up catching a venereal disease which I was cured of *very fast*. After I caught the disease I started to do some real thinking. I realized that sex wasn't the most important thing in life. *Please* forgive me for what I did in the Navy. The reason I went to the prostitutes when I was in the Navy was because of my shyness. It didn't matter that I was shy with these girls. All they wanted was my money. *Please* forgive me for what I did in the Navy.

I have tried writing to girls as pen pals. I even met two girls this way. It hasn't worked out. *Please* believe me I just can't get rid of this shyness. I feel so desperate and lonely right now. I feel like I am going crazy. *Please* don't think I'm a nut and *Please* believe this letter. . . .

If you write back, please don't tell me to go where girls are. I'm afraid to go to those places. I really am *afraid*. . . .

I don't know what to do anymore. I *can't* get a girlfriend. I feel so lonely. Lately I have been thinking about going to a prostitute in this area. I've been thinking about paying her to just talk to me. I figure if I can *really* learn to talk to her I can talk to other girls. I wouldn't have sexual intercourse with her. . . .

If you write, *Please* don't give me any advice because it won't work with me. I'm writing this letter to ask you if you can somehow, someway fix me up with a date with some girl from around the Pittsburgh area. . . .

28

If you can help me I'll owe my life to you. I would *really appreciate* it if you could help me. Please try to help me. I'm going to put a picture of myself in the letter. It might help you in trying to get me a date.

Let me tell you about myself. It might help you in picking out someone for me. I work as a maintenance man at a storage company. I will never get rich. I don't drive and I never want to get a driver's license. I also live with my folks.

I've decided to put $20.00 in this letter to try and prove to you that this letter is the *truth*. Please believe the letter and please try to help me.

PS: You can *keep* the money whether you can help me or not. I've put a self addressed envelope in the letter. I really am *terribly lonely*.

Sam's letter contained a dimestore photo of a young man with glasses. The envelope also included a self-addressed envelope and a twenty-dollar bill. I wrote to him several times. We sent back his money and tried to encourage him to call me. There was a counselor friend who would be glad to work with him. This letter raises the problem that I struggled with so often. Should we try to relate people with similar needs? This question has been answered in the negative. We simply can't process people into relationship patterns from the limited input we have. I can refer folks to counseling help. This works in many cases. People actually follow these recommendations.

9:19—Man calls to complain about his treatment following his military experience. He was wounded in the war and is still in the hospital. The veteran does not feel accepted by society. He suspects that his chances for the future are poor. He sounds depressed.

Dear Mr. Benson,

On the air Sunday, a fellow called about his troubles since he returned from the war. I'd like it very much if you'd forward this letter to him. He's right. It is and will be hard and I guess he's paid his dues for the war—but as for people looking down on him, I think not—I mean really negative people don't or maybe shouldn't look down on another for their beliefs.

It will be hard getting a job maybe, but that's the price you pay—especially when it's as expensive as physical ability. You yourself get down on yourself—you have to be optimistic even when times get rough, because optimism and hope in yourself will practically be the only things keeping you going.

I know what I am talking about. This is how I am making it. I have been handicapped since birth. It gets trying and lonely sometimes. However, you can overcome. . . .

PS: Please excuse my crude scribbling.

It is our style to identify emotionally with the caller or writer as much as possible. We affirm the human attributes and try not to minimize the real or imagined handicap. *Rap Around* gained a large audience of mentally and physically disadvantaged persons. When a caller would talk with a stutter and strange speech pattern, I never challenged the person. We assumed that people call to exchange personhood. I could afford to be made the fool. However, not one person should ever be placed in a position of possible embarrassment through a challenge of credibility.

Dear M.R. Benson,

I am in need of help I have to have someone to talk to I am so desperate I don't know where to turn I am 26 years old and am trap in this house with no way out I think I will kill my self. No one cares about me right now I am crying so heard to make matters worse I fell in love with a boy that made a compleat fool out of me He told me that he love me and cuase I needed love so bad I fell for it no one love me not even my mother she says I am a retard that is all I have been hearing all my life Everyone says that since nothing but bad has happen to me for 26 years that the good will come but when I am tired of wateing I tryed to be like my brothers and sisters I realy did but I couldn't make it why dosn't anybody love me

I live with my grand mother and grand father what I can't understand why my mother gave me away like I said she dosn't love me nobody dose. My grandfather is the one that keep me lock up I don't know why I can't go no ware by my self if I go out it has to be with them. . . . I am so dam tird I don't know where to turn I realy think if I kill myself no one would even miss me

I would love to get married some day but who would have me I can't even function as a woman. I had some thing I wanted to know about sex but forget it when I went to my mother she said I was to young to know so I set out to fine my own answewer then that how I was made a fool of I feel so dead inside I am all ready dead all I have to do is lay down do you ever feel so empty inside that you could die that's me like I said I am all ready dead I just have to lay down so I just will do what I must and not bother you or anyone else   thanks for the shoulder to cry on. . . .

M.R. Benson,
    Thanks for your kind letter it helps a littel to know you care you say be of good cheer well I am trying but mean time life go's on and is seem so hopeless my grandfather read your letter to me

he read it but he didn't understand it things are worst then ever he was so mad that I wrote he broke the chair. M.R. Benson you know and I know that I need to be around other people but how do we make them understand I have tryed to tell them that not all people are bad like I told you before my grand parents has told me for the past 26 years that I am retarded and the people will take advantage of me maybe so but I can't worry about that M.R. Benson there a grate big world out there and I just have to be part of it I didn't tell you every thing in my last letter that the phones in this house are lock that is because the boy I used to date my grandparents didn't like him or any boy I went with he wants to put me up on a petastaul and worship me I don't want to be worship if you handle me I won't brake the boy I date now wants me to marry him I think he says that cause he feels sorry for me I don't want his simpthany I am not ready for marage just yet I haven't live yet I told him that and he said he would wate as long as he has to but how long he will have to I don't know maybe forever so thank again and please put me in touch with your friends cause I need bad to relate to other people I would marry Peter to get out of this house but that wouldn't be fair to him but I do love him I think. . . .

Marcia Miscall, my seminarian colleague at the time, pored over Pam's letters with me. We were consoling each other as we felt waves of pain and resentment. Such a sensitive girl. Why couldn't she be permitted to pursue some sort of normal life? We picked apart the crudely written notes. Her intuitions for survival are frighteningly perceptive. She really knows the basic quality needed for true humanity—community. This is something most "normal" people in the culture cannot appreciate. The way she deals with the balance between her responsibility and the need for freedom is stable and fair. Her thoughts are clearly etched. The slips of grammar and punctuation cannot disguise a fine ability of self-exploration and articulation. Yet, she remains a prisoner of other people's fear and limitations. Marcia wanted to go to the girl's house and confront the situation. In moments of deeper reflection we tearfully accepted the fact that our contract of communication left the burden of action to the other. We were there to respond in what ways that we could. Pam was given a contact.

Dear Mr. Benson,

It's great that somebody cares enough to give people the chance to really rap about what they honestly think and feel. . . . Anyway, the problem is that I can't get a job, my parents are mad at me, and I am really getting restless. I do things around the house, but I have to get out of here. I am home on vacation from college.

I have put an application in all the department stores in downtown Pittsburgh. I have applied for everything from sales clerk to clerical billing. They all said that they are not hiring right now. In one store, the receptionist put my name on a piece of paper and she told me to come back in three weeks. That's the same thing she told me twice before. When I left, I noticed she filed my name in the waste-basket.

I neglected to tell you I am handicapped. I am not holding that against myself or anyone because it really isn't anyone's fault. I was just born a year or so too early for Mr. Salk to do his work. Anyway, I feel that personality is more important than physical traits or deformities. Obviously, personnel directors don't agree.

I get along pretty good, I'm slow, but eventually I reach my destination. I'm also not the

33

brightest person around. My friends have told me that I have a nice personality because I try to keep smiling as much as I can. Unfortunately, that smile isn't the winning kind. I still don't have a job.

My parents don't actually help either. My so-called mother has actually come out and said she knew I wouldn't get a job. I must admit it hurts pretty bad.

My question is, how can I get a job and how can I get people to accept me for what I am *inside?* Especially my mother (written in ink).

Thanks so much just for letting me write to you. It seems to help when I am able just to write it all down. . . .

Dear Jan,

. . . My heart particularly goes out to you concerning the dilemma you're now facing. Times are extremely tight and so many of my friends are having a difficult time getting a job. . . .

I can understand how you feel concerning some of the interviews. People are particularly cruel and insensitive about any variation in a person's appearance or gifts. I get bad vibes from my hair and beard. . . .

I was lucky enough to get polio after Mr. Salk's vaccine was developed. It laid me up for a few months in the hospital, but didn't leave me with any bad effects. Having been so close to what you are enduring, I have particularly strong feelings concerning you and what you are facing. . . .

Don't put yourself down. You are a person and you are therefore dear and important. Inner qualities of love and courage shine through your letter. Don't be unduly influenced by the snap judgments of the world. People easily make conclusions on the early returns concerning a person's success or failure. It is the long stretch which really counts.

I do have one source of a job. Betty Jouran is a friend of mine who has been successful in getting some of my friends jobs for the summer. Call her and tell her that I told you to call. She is the kind of person who is not put off by appearances.

The greatest gift we have to give to people is love—a love that reaches out and changes events and other people. Keep developing and nurturing the love you so richly possess. Help your parents be more loving and enable them to fulfill their role. . . .

Jan got her job and she continues to meet her struggles. There will be many to face. However, her gift to life will be much.

9:23—A high school student calls in with critical comments about the President. He is very angry and makes a lot of wild charges.

. . . "If I had a gun, I would kill him."

"Wow . . . That is pretty heavy . . . I can understand where you are coming from . . . I don't dig him either. However, it doesn't help much just to agree in our mutual despair. Let's use our imaginations. . . . Suppose I could turn him over to you for a couple days. . . ."

". . . I would fix him. . . ."

". . . No, I mean that you were in the thought process of the future. It is your job to recondition him to be the kind of person you think we need in the presidency."

"Ya . . . that is hard. . . . I think that I would get him into music. Ya . . . he needs to open his head to some sounds which would free up his body and head. Maybe we could start with some Grand Funk [we laugh]. That sure would clean out his sinuses [more laughter]. Next I would expose him to some James Taylor or Joni

Mitchell. Ya . . . that would be nice. After he had heard the stuff for five or six hours I would take him to the beach. Mess up his hair and make him walk barefooted in the wet sand of a beach . . . Or we could lie on our backs and just look at the clouds for a couple hours . . . Maybe I could give him a backrub and get those fascist knots and kinks out of his body . . ."

We rap on for a couple minutes. The tightness and anger subside a bit. We put fantasy in place of sharing futility. This may not be the best or only way of dealing with political impotency. However, this flight of the mind broadened our range of human capability.

Dear Mr. Benson,
   I hope that I got your name right. Last night while I was listening to your show, I wasn't sure if that was your name, as I was only able to listen for about twenty minutes. Getting down to brass tacks, I really didn't like your show. Not that it isn't well run, and you are not a good host, I just didn't like most of the views expressed. I don't mean you don't have the right to express these views, I just think you come on a little strong. Here's the real clincher.
   I would like to appear on your show if it would be at all possible. I would like to give a conservative viewpoint that isn't coming from a 68 year old Senator, but from a fifteen year old high school student . . . I feel that you may find the "tribe" as you call them are not as liberal as you may think. So, I hope that your answer will be yes. . . .

Dear Edward,
   Thank you very much for your recent letter. You did, indeed, get my name correctly spelled. I'm sorry that you weren't able to hear more of the show. I think I do come on strong in certain

matters. This is the kind of show it is supposed to be. Yet, nobody crams anybody's viewpoint down people's throats. *Rap Around* is an opportunity to express our feelings about all kinds of issues. You're welcome to call in and present the kinds of views that you really feel.

I'm sorry you missed the first hour-and-a-half of the show. In the course of that hour we had a policeman call and a couple servicemen. The conversation with these people was very important to me. We're not trying to express simply my viewpoint on issues. *Rap Around* is an opportunity to express human feelings about what we believe. I am convinced that we can disagree and yet be part of the same community.

I do not indeed assume that our community or tribe is liberal. In fact, I have difficulty understanding the labels, "liberal" and "conservative." I think there are simply people with varying positions on certain aspects of life.

We don't use guests at all. However, I would be delighted to have a deeper conversation with you. Would it be possible for you to appear on my other program *The Place*, which is broadcast on the station Sunday mornings? I am the host of this hour long format. There is no pre-determined direction or control concerning the conversation and it could go anywhere that you might desire.

Thank you once again for your letter. I appreciate the concern which has compelled you to write to me. I hope that you will call in on *Rap Around* and express the opinions which are closest to your concern. I care about you and respect the commitment which enables you to pursue your beliefs. . . .

Edward and I did several *Place* shows together. He was nervous and fearful during our first meeting. It seemed that he expected someone who would try to devour him with "liberalism." However, our relationship became quite trusting over the course of these shows!

Dear Mr. Benson,

I listened to part of your show the other night. I came into the room and my son was engrossed in a conversation you were having with a weirdo who was going to brutalize our President with rock music. As I listened further, I couldn't believe what I heard. All kinds of discussions about sex and race were on the program. How can your station permit such discussion on the air? My son is only 14 and I don't want him to hear such things. . . .

PS: Please don't let my son know that I am writing.

Dear Mr. Watts,

Thank you for your letter of concern. I can appreciate the kinds of worries you have about your son facing the kind of world we live in. Our show represents a cross-section of our community. Many people are thinking, doing, and discussing things which may be frightening to all of us.

We really care about the young people and adults of our community. Love and concern are the qualities we nurture each week. We are simply willing to meet the audience wherever it wants to be. We don't introduce topics. The caller suggests the focus.

I know that you really care about this matter. I would like to talk to you personally. Why don't you come down to the station some Sunday evening and observe our operation firsthand? We could talk over coffee. Call me if you will accept my invitation. You are welcome to bring your son. . . .

Dear Dennis,

I hope you are sincere. I listen to your program infrequently.

My purpose in writing to you is to relate to you my experiences in the last year as an aware being. You can use it as you see fit, but maybe it will help somebody, somewhere to realize he or she is not so alone as the person may assume.

I started college after being super-fanatically involved with the Presidential campaign. I had all these idealistic visions of what a beautiful world we could make, if everybody would just relate to each other. At the time I still believed in the "democratic" system. Hippies were beautiful and I loved everybody. I was involved in the campaign. I let my classes slide. The war protests took more time from class. But while I was involved politically, I was also emotionally caught up with people that Middle America calls hippies, commies, perverts, etc.

I feel for people, I'm sensitive. I caught the brunt of all the insults my friends were getting. I myself was called all kinds of really unbelievable things for being around my Afro friends. And I hurt and I was wounded and the wound never was allowed to heal and just festered and grew.

Then the kids started getting killed and gassed and I cried and didn't smile as much as before. I began to worry about us. All my friends became very quiet when we got together. Then came Kent and more anti-war action. Kids I knew turned from love and peace and said if they don't listen to us on our terms, let's give it to them on theirs—killing, hate, and violence. So we went to a local university and broke into the ROTC building and tried to burn it down. I was very scared. I could see my people becoming all that we so abhorred. I never went to class and finally I was dismissed. I was out of everything.

Now I have a job, full time and I'm going to school part time in order to be reinstated. I've talked to some of my friends from before and we've grown apart. They're quiet and very brooding. They are filled with hate. I thought we were a peaceful and loving people.

So you see, it's just all so futile. You can't get too involved or what happened to me will ruin you. But then if you manage to hack the hostile approach, you get to *be* the enemy. Like "Lord of the Flies."

Why? How? When? I don't know. I do know I'm afraid, afraid for not only freaks, kids, straight and old folks, but for everyone. . . .

Dear Marge,

Thank you very much for your important letter. You so willingly shared so much of yourself. It really hit me hard. I have also been through some of the hassles you've experienced. I guess I've been at it a little longer than you. My whole bag includes Selma, Milwaukee, Chicago, and Washington, D.C. I have done the whole tutoring, marching, and campus scene. In fact, I was fired from a campus job because of my organization work with black students.

I was also disturbed to see my friends turning to violence and making bombs. It is a heavy scene. I am much like you. I can't quite strike that opponent because he's intolerant and hostile.

I've got to be frank and tell you that I feel basically hopeful. I feel that I must authentically give of myself and stand for what is right and be willing to pay the price. I think that in some sense I may have to be willing to give up my life for what I believe is justice and truth. I am called to do and be in spite of the chance for success. We have no choice. We must live out our commitment to love and peace even in a hopeless environment.

I only hope that all of us can keep it together and not just withdraw. There is a strong temptation in the face of disillusionment to withdraw and indeed become that which we are fighting.

I am commited to loving both straight America and my friends in resistance. I love both the uptight middle American types and the strung out former revolutionary freak. They're both my brothers and sisters. In them rests my essence and my hope. . . .

Dear Dennis,

Wow, I'm really psyched that you answered my letter. I guess you are for real after all. You see so few really sincere people nowdays that it is really hard to relate them to reality. . . .

I have been out of school for some time. I work every day. I'm not a secretary, I'm a salesgirl. I see and talk to Mrs. Householder. My views have been tempered by the expression of genuine fear for the nation's people.

I also talk with kids who are in school. These folks are not former revolutionaries. They are children of our times. They haven't been through the late sixties. They are not bitter like my bomb-prone friends. They are just frozen. They don't care about anybody, but themselves. These new plastic models only worry about their future job, their booze, and sex. In a sense they are worse than Mrs. Householder. Perhaps I am just getting old. It hasn't taken very long for me to be from another era.

Dennis, I am very afraid. I haven't seen it all yet. I'm sure I'm going to live through alot more. I feel the way you do. I am honestly willing to give everything in my power, including my life to make things more balanced in our nation's life. As you well know, it is awfully lonesome in this state between these several groups. And I'm very small. Be happy. . . .

PS: Hang in there, yourself. We need you. . . .

Dear Marge,

. . . Maybe we can only huddle together in the midst of the cold and get intellectual and spiritual warmth from each other. I hope that we can develop a style that enables us to deal with that which is less than successful and yet stand up because of its authenticity. . . .

. . . Hang in there, sister. I'm glad that you are grasping for a concept of celebration. May you be blessed with joy. Be of good cheer. . . .

9:28—Rap about sending letters if the listener can't get on the air with call. Station I.D.

A small knot of kids has gathered outside the windows. They can hear the show through the speakers which are mounted on the outside of the building. They push against the huge expanse of glass. I turn and wave to them. There are some familiar faces. Joanne is there. She always seems to be sitting in front of the station. What a confused life she has. She has been into drugs, sex, and just about everything that would un-nerve the local school marm. She spends every spare moment in front of those windows.

It is important to acknowledge pleasantly those who stand outside the window. If you turn and say something to someone else in the studio or laugh, it is easy for the person who can't hear to suspect that you are talking about him or her. When someone reacts to another so that the response is seen but not heard, the process of communication can be scrambled easily. A disc jockey was shot at while he was on the air. Someone became angry at reactions he interpreted as being hostile. At any rate, Joanne needs all the strokes she can get. She is a very sensitive person and writes poetry. Pat often spends time counseling her after the program. He certainly is a loving guy. I feel so lucky to have him as the phone producer.

My body is quite tight. I have got to loosen up. The tension will start showing in my voice. It is easiest to listen to many of the calls with my eyes closed. Our mouths and ears are actually inches apart. There is a sense in which *Rap Around* becomes an electronic confessional. What a strange mixture of imagery. Imagine confessing before the widest possible audience! Yet, the caller is protected from discovery and identification. There is also a payoff in getting something out which has not or cannot be shared in other ways. Perhaps it is "cheap" pardon, I don't know. The theological means of grace may function only in a derived sense; however, I am thankful for what we do have.

9:29—A thirteen-year-old boy calls about the trouble he is having in his neighborhood. The other boys are calling him names and saying that he is a sissy. He is interested in music and art. He asks if there is something wrong with him.

> *"Hello Dennis . . . My problem is about male ballet dancers. I have been thinking about taking ballet lessons, but I'm afraid that taking ballet lessons just wouldn't hit it off just right with my friends and the family. My reasons for thinking about ballet are thus:*
> *a. The dance fascinates and intrigues me.*
> *b. It is said that taking ballet helps in a person's poise and also helps to have better coordination in many sport activities.*

c. I may have a chance at the ballet company in Pittsburgh which I have heard is quite a good organization.

"There are also cons of taking ballet. First of all, I don't think the kids at school would care to associate with a male ballet dancer. Most of the high school age boys don't take too kindly to a boy who as they say "puts on tights and prances around a dance floor." Girl friends also would laugh and call a boy a "sissy" or various other things that aren't too becoming to males.

"I just don't know what to do. It seems I'm stuck in the middle of a circle. You see, there are some of my friends who sympathize with me. But, it seems that all my friends are just talk and no action. I thought that if I could get another kid to go along and take lessons with me, I could make it. I was going to ask a kid who is involved in a local folk dance troup to switch to ballet, but he says no dice. What should I do? Hang up the tights and go back to flared jeans (and an old shirt) or go dancing. . . ."

The caller did most of the talking. He seemed very sensitive and mature. He could balance the situation quite well. His friends were into baseball and other sports. The student seemed to recognize that in the mill town where he lived there was a tracking system for the youth. The schools with community support rewarded sports achievements with acclaim. Yet, he knew that this was a dead-end system. Old local sports stars who lived in the town were still working in the mill and driving their old cars. The listener conjectured that his community was simply distracting the young people from the fact that there was no future to such preparation. Academic and art interests received no affirmation from the community.

As we talked, I was struck by his ability to think out the

problem. In fact, most of the listeners and writers frequently come up with a good analysis of their situations. It was almost the process of telling which made situations clear to them. They were sometimes surprised at their own insights.

My brother at the other end of the phone projects his situation over the kind of life his father was experiencing. These attributes of being a man seemed so shallow to him.

> *"He drinks a lot of beer with the boys. He always takes his paycheck to the same bar on the way home from work. When he is with his friends, they seem to spend most of their time talking about previous drinking occasions. He falls asleep before the television set. We also have several hunting guns around the house. He never goes hunting. He just plays with them. I love him. However, his life is so empty. There are moments in our arguments when I catch an expression in his eyes which acknowledges that he knows I am right. Yet, he certainly resents me and everything I appreciate. It is hard to fight upstream against my friends and family. I guess that I am a person in the wrong place at the wrong time. Thanks, for rapping, Dennis. I wish you were my brother."*

Dear Mr. Benson,

I have a problem that I consider quite complex. First of all, let me give you some information about myself. I am a 10th grade student and in an advanced program. I live with foster parents (not legal foster parents) in a small apartment (which adds to my problem), 15 years of age and a homosexual (which is my problem).

There is no doubt in my mind I am a homosexual, because I have a male "lover" who is 25 years old and is presently in prison till his sentence ends in about eight months. I know to someone straight like you, this may all sound very bizarre, but I think you are a very open-minded person.

You must understand that homosexuals are in the minority, but by no way are homosexuals "abnormal," and neither is homosexuality. This is a scientific fact. It is different but not "abnormal."

Howard, my lover, and I are very devoted to each other. I know that he would not cheat on me. Sex is not an important factor of our relationship, but love. Love meaning that I would give my life for him and he would give his life for me. I will stand by him and he will stand by me in all situations.

We have had long discussions to see if we are really ment for each other and not making a mistake and we came to the conclusion we are not. We have made plans for the future, and are going to put those plans into actions as soon as he gets on his feet and I am completely done with my education.

My problem is social. I met Howard while I was still in junior high school and at that time, the story leaked out. I don't know how. These 3 girls who are supposed to be my friends spread it around in school. Not everyone in my high school knows, but I'm afraid they may find out.

I have to go there for three more years. I enter into no social activities, make no friends because of this fear and this is making my grades decline and greatly effecting me emotionally.

Not only do I worry about the school kids finding out, but most of all, my parents. All I need is for them to find out and I know they would reject me instantly, as they have definite and set ideas on this subject. They do not suspect anything yet. Once while I brought up the subject, they said they would completely have nothing to do with me if they found out I was a homosexual. This wouldn't be hard for them to do as they have no legal ties with me and don't have the parent-son feeling for me. They have had me since I was three. If they make me leave, I would have to go to my father. I keep in contact with him and we are not perfect strangers, but it would be impossible to communicate with him about this.

. . . I'm also afraid to face the future. Homosexuals are greatly discriminated against and almost completely rejected from society. Society and the United States is geared to the heterosexual culture. I believe things will get worse before they get better due to the "Gay Liberation." This scares me to death. I don't want to be forced to associate only with homosexuals, but all cultures and peoples.

My problem is learning how to accept being tramped on, rejected, hated and socially not accepted in general. Homosexuality is a much more touchy problem than race, religion and politics put together.

Even religion rejects homosexuals by calling us "an abomination to God" (from the Bible). I have found a deep place with God and He has been a great hope and help. With Him I have Howard. These two make a great team in helping me to survive and accept the inevitable. Society is made up of many different parts. It can't function without wholeness. What I am saying is, even though I have God and Howard, I can not survive. I need the society with the majority of peoples to accept me. Without them I will exist, with them God and Howard, I will survive. Since they will not accept me, how can I accept to merely exist? This is my problem.

If you want to help me, please do. If you do not, believe me I will truly understand. Because of your position I know your hands are tied. I will not blame it on you but society, because if society would accept me, I would not have to come to you for help and you wouldn't have to decline. If helping me may effect your character, please don't. I don't mean you'll turn "gay" helping me, because I have absolutely no designs on you, but I worry what people would think if they found out, which is very unlikely.

If you decide to help me, I believe a person to person talk would help more. I know you are a very busy man and it is asking a lot of you, but if it is at all possible, please consider it. If you can, please give me a call between 4:00 and 7:30 P.M. Thank you. . . .

Jerome came to my office a week later. He was carefully dressed. He moved and spoke in the same thoughtful manner as he wrote. It was easy to talk because I had dropped him a note.

Dear Jerome,

. . . I'm very interested in the questions you raise concerning your life and thought. As you may have caught from the show, I have several friends who are in similar situations.

My view on life is that each person is to be known and understood according to his or her worth as a person. I think the things you expressed in your letter concerning life and love are very important and real. I can also appreciate how such a concern leaves you in quite a sense of tension.

Let's talk. Call my office. I agree that it would be better for us to talk in person. Thank you for your concern and trust. I'll look forward to hearing from you. . . .

We talked a long time. Jerome was clear about his life. He even seemed to have a better grip on things than indicated in his letter. We were not there to debate homosexuality. He was isolated without a significant other. I could and did affirm his personhood and his quality of love. After two hours, he seemed very relaxed. We had gone over the kinds of trials facing him and Howard in our society again. He thanked me for listening. He thought he could now continue to face the tension of the present and future. We would talk again.

When I received the bag of mail containing Jerome's letter, we had company from the West Coast. Mary is an educator who has contributed a lot to the open class-room concept in public education. I opened some of the letters as we sat in a restaurant. I read sections of Jerome's letter to Mary and my wife, Marilyn. Our guest asked what I was going to do. I told her that I would see him and how I was concerned about him as a person. Mary then told us she was a lesbian. We spent many hours talking with her about the struggles she has faced in her field. Public education just doesn't understand her defini-tion of her sexuality.

Being a significant other demands that we retain who we are. There is no room for those who become whatever the other person is. However, there is great freedom in this role to permit the other person to be whomever he or she may reveal. It is striking how open and honest people are waiting to be. It is the social veneer of appear-ance which keeps us apart from each other. It is possible to love and care for someone with a different sexual orientation without changing perspective. It may be pain-ful to anticipate the hurt which the society will inflict upon him or her. However, this is the same emotional crunch we experience on behalf of anyone we love. Our care can easily become possession. We want to control where the loved ones will conclude their pondering and actualization of values. The significant other is not afforded this kind of luxury. It is a relationship of enabling which provides a human circle of probing in which possibilities may only be dimly gleaned.

9:33—Widower calls to talk about the loneliness of his life. He feels trapped by the social structure and himself.

... *"It has been difficult since my wife died. I have three children to care for. This lady takes care of them during the day. I feel that I should give them as much time as possible in the evenings and weekends. There has been no time to seek the companionship of a woman. . . ."*

"... You mean, it is hard to make contact with someone who could be a companion?"

"Well, I did go to a parents group. You know, it was one of those groups for parents that don't have partners living or in the home. I just couldn't stand it. Everyone seemed to be looking for husbands or wives . . . Well, maybe that isn't fair . . . I have been kind of shy about dating again. It has been two years since my wife died. I don't know . . . it is just hard. . . ."

"Ya. . . . A lot of feelings surface when we face a situation like this."

"Ya, I am going through a lot of feelings. I wish I had the occasion to meet women so that I could get used to the dating kind of relationship once again. There simply isn't any way to meet such women . . . I am lonely and feel kind of lost. . . ."

Hi Mr. Benson,

I'm not a good writer. Hope you can make this letter out. Mr. Benson, I'm a widow. My husband passed on—it will be 5 years this April.

I am white and respectable and lonely. Too

50

bad there is no place so a person could go and meet some nice gentleman. Would you know some nice respectable man so he could write me? I do not drink or smoke or gamble. I'm Catholic and if there is any place you have to pay or if you are on social security and the money is limited, you cannot go too far with rent to pay with what I get. At my age I can not get a job. No one will hire me.

On social security you get $68.00. You can not pay rent, medicine, food, and clothing. When a person is diabetic, it sure costs a person so you can not do very much.

What is wrong with these men you hear about that just want to go and stay with a woman? What is coming off anymore? They all tell you the same thing. Only motel and hotel. I lived with my husband 42 years and never heard such filth. What is going on today? I'm sure there are some decent people yet. . . .

PS: I am 62 years old.

Dear Dennis,

. . . I am eighteen years old and am seeking some personal help from you. Last fall, I went away to college and within a few weeks, I was back home in an almost suicidal behavior. Accumulating circumstances and situations mistakenly convinced me that I could not cope in the situation I put myself in, at that time. I retreated back to my home to give myself time to receive some professional help with a social worker. In the meantime, I have finished extensive counseling with a very dedicated social worker, taken a full-time job and enrolled in the local school part-time.

My problem is establishing relationships with new people my own age. I have almost completely broken with my limited former high school associates and have little desire to re-develop relationships with them. My desire is to meet new people and to "try to get it on" with them instead of being "depressively lonely" as I am now.

A probable hypothesis of yours might be that I am very difficult to get along with or that I am very particular with whom I associate. I have given this much thought and found that it is not true since I enjoy being with the people I work with. The problem is that they are much my elder.

Can you direct me to an organization that can be of assistance to me in this nature? Did you ever ask someone out and find out that she is old enough to be your parents' friend? I am most interested in relating to some young women my age. . . .

Dear Mr. Benson

I am an eighteen year old girl and very much alone, alienated, and abandoned. Yet, somewhat ironically, I am living comfortably in suburbia. I go to night school, have a good job, can buy what I want and am generally well set. Somehow though, I do not feel happy and I am constantly depressed, terribly pessimistic and forever melancholy.

I can't seem to find anyone I like as far as men go. I am afraid that I am going to lose out on love. I don't see any joy in life because my parents aren't suited for each other because my father is a weak-spined man and my mother dreads the day when all of us kids get married and leave her alone with my boring father. . . .

I really do like people, but for years I have been plagued by my bashfulness and my inferiorities. I frequently feel that my journalistic pursuit will never materialize because I don't feel confident in my abilities. Yet, I have always done quite well in English and what's more, I have a terrible craving to write.

I am concerned about the world and its problems. Yet, there is that selfish aspect of me—me and my paranoid inferiorities. I don't feel right because I'm flat-chested. Don't laugh, friend. I don't feel normal because I have very few friends and no place to meet new people.

It somehow feels as though it is far too late to make friends, to have a half-decent figure (don't laugh), to find someone I love, to become a writer, to remold my personality into something, to help my parents improve the quality of their lives, etc.

I had joy once when I was young and free. But now there are so many responsibilities left to me. And I have learned that life is no romance, so why am I to be joyful? I am so alone.

PS: I don't cop out on anything—I don't smoke, take drugs, drink, or engage in premarital sex. . . .

There are so many lonely people. Even those who have found the shelter of a relationship are not protected by the experience when death or separation takes place. It is easy to be angry about the depersonalization of the urban complex. The churches, clubs, and social institutions are designed for couples and families. Yet, what keeps these folks from reaching out?

As I talked with the man who had lost his wife I mentally projected myself in the same situation. Could I reestablish the rhythm of dating and companionship if I were suddenly snatched from the security and warmth of my present love setting? It is always hard for me to find conversational friends on the road. The giving and receiving of hospitality is difficult. The lonely folks listening to *Rap Around* tonight probably contribute to their own problems. Strangers would say that this lonely widower isn't very friendly to others. Shyness so often projects the mask of silent hostility.

This man is now on the phone. He is probably confessing

things about his life that he has never said to anyone. We can't touch him because he will be able to slip back into his silent defense posture 'as he faces others tomorrow. Does he need more counseling? Perhaps it will be wise to have him call me after the show for referral. Getting a person to some real counseling always seems to work better if I can make a private recommendation. It seems most successful if I can suggest someone who is a friend. This is a good way to transfer the person's trust in me to the counselor. It is also the only way we can function in the city. We can't make blanket recommendations for social service agencies. Some of the counselors in a given institution are good with some people while others are not. One friend asked me not to send any teenagers to her. "I simply don't get along with them." I respect this kind of honesty.

> "Call George," I said. "He is a beautiful guy. We are good friends. He is into music and media. You should see some of the sound and slides and things he has done. Beautiful. Call him and tell him that Dennis told you to call. He will take good care of you when he knows that you are a friend of mine. If there is any hassle, give me a call. Call again, anyway. I want to know how things are going with you."

Such referred situations occur often. I know that I can't personally counsel the *Rap Around* folk. The press of the people would wipe me out. They also know that our contract for phone conversation is only on Sundays. Letters can be sent and will be answered anytime.

The slender thread connecting some people to the source of help became apparent when we suggested that a particular teenager call a friend at a counseling service.

> *"Hey, man. I called your friend. But I didn't*

talk to him. When I called, a woman answered the phone. She was real hard. She had a real put-down voice. It was just bad vibes. I hung up. . . ."

The referral process also works in a different direction. One Sunday evening before we went on the air we got a call from a teenager who had been deeply into a drug problem. We had encouraged him to visit a drug center near his home. He was calling to get my assurance about the counselor's suggestion that he be taken to the hospital right then. We rapped about the feelings he had.

"I am afraid that they will never let me out. I don't want to be in a bug house forever. . . ."

". . . What did Joe tell you about the hospitalization?"

"He said that it would only be for a few days. He said that I needed some tests and medication . . . he is right. I am pretty bummed out right now. What do you think, Dennis? I told them I would not go until I talked with you. . . ."

I talked with the counselor for a couple minutes. I then assured my friend on the bad trip that it was okay. We arranged it so that he could call me from the hospital. He went and they were able to get him together—for this crisis anyway.

As I sit and take these calls, it is overwhelming all over again to feel the trust people extend to me. There is no reason for this kind of faith. Nothing very wise and important has been said by me this evening. Part of this instant power comes from the medium. This station is the top rocker in town. After twelve hours of solid music comes *Rap Around.* Just being near the music gives one good will and access to the possibility of becoming a significant other.

Dear Mr. Benson,

I am in trouble. I am 26 and have four children. Everything in this house is caving in on me. I just can't take it any longer. I go through periods of time when my whole world becomes black. I get so depressed that I want to kill myself. I know that I am going to do it.

I am Catholic. The priest does not understand. There is no one. *Please* help me.

My letter to Sheila urged her to contact my friends at an excellent counseling center. She was also invited to call me at home if for some reason she couldn't make contact. Four or five weeks went by. One evening about 11:00 she called my home in a panic. She said that she had not made the counseling contact. The walls were again closing in on her and she was afraid that she was going to take her life that night.

I assured her that she would not do this. I told her that she was reaching out for help and this indicated to me that she could be helped. She calmed down. I underscored the fact that she needed counseling and now could be helped. Calling me was a positive sign that she was ready to seek a way out of her depression. I told her to call me at 10:00 in the morning and that I would have made all the arrangements for her to get help the same day. She was encouraged to call me anytime in the night if she became scared.

I have often relived that night. It had been my instant hunch that she trusted me. Being on radio, I was a person bigger than life. If she had known me, it might not have worked. However, here was a person for whom it had been proven (as a faithful listener) that I could help people. If I affirmed the fact that she could hold on, then it must be so. In other words, I risked that I might become a significant other in a special way. It was a long night. In the morning I called the center and was able to cut through the red tape. They promised to be standing by to make an appointment for her that day. With this center such a responsive action was unusual. Most community institutions are particularly responsive when you call from a newspaper, radio, or television station.

Sheila called at 10:00. She was calm and collected. Her appointment went through well. We talked again about six months later. She was still in counseling. There were still some bad moments. However, she felt that she now had enough strength to make it through these valleys of depression. This hunch was risky. It may have been dangerous. However, trust is a commodity which few professions or institutions enjoy. The significant other is often endowed with trust beyond that which she or he deserves. It is the cautious and sensitive return of this trust which can make the relationship so important.

9:36—Girl calls in to discuss a call on last week's show. A pregnant teenager had called in and talked over the pros and cons of getting an abortion. This week's caller is against abortion.

"Please tell me what gives anyone the right to kill anyone else? Why does anyone think that just because you can't see someone's face that they don't exist? I just wish an unborn child could be consulted before it is aborted.

"If a person can't handle the responsibilities of parenthood, they should not do anything to put themselves in a position to have a child. I am a Catholic but I would take birth control if the population was really out of hand when I get married. But I would never murder an innocent child.

"I just wonder what an unborn child would

say if they were asked, 'Honey, I don't want to get married or tied down, so can I have an abortion to get rid of you?' Everyone no matter how old has the right to life.

"Kids shouldn't get themselves in the situation where they are pregnant. It is just foolish. They deserve the troubles they get. . . ."

Dear Denny,

My parents and I got into a big hassle about 3 months ago over this guy. I've been dating him for four months. My parents met him and they thought he was a real creep. Well, this is what the fight was about which led to my leaving home.

I am presently living with my very best girl-friend. Annie is 22. Well, I was getting fed up so one night my man came over and spent the night while Annie was out of town and we did it all the way. Now I have to face an unwanted pregnancy. I can't go home and face my parents. They will say that they told me it would happen.

The father of the child doesn't want to admit to it and as I stand now neither do I. I don't think I'm emotionally and physically up to this pregnancy. It is so terrible because I'm only 19 and not even married.

Annie is really a great kid who is still a virgin and is so understanding of me, but I'm still all alone anyway. I'm sorry I took so much of your time, but I feel a lot better in my heart now that I've told you. Please answer this letter. . . .

Dear Mr. Benson,

I have a problem that really isn't my problem, but it bothers me deeply. It has to do with my roommate.

Well, my roommate, Karen, is pregnant. We are very close and this is why I know. She has a boyfriend and they love each other very much. But this is ruining their lives. Her boyfriend,

Mason, wants to marry her and she wants to marry him, but she refuses now that she is pregnant. She wants an abortion and Mason is willing to let her get one. However, they don't have the money. Even if she married Mason now, she still doesn't want the baby. She is going to school and wants to become a dancer. If she doesn't get through school and have a career, she swears it will kill her.

What is worse, if she has this baby it may be deformed because she has taken so many pills, hoping that they would cause a miscarriage. Why I am worried even now is that last Friday she tried to commit suicide. Last Wednesday she took five different kinds of pills. 24 tablets in all. But she vomited it all up and she didn't get too sick. You just can't believe how shook up she is over this and I'm afraid if something doesn't happen soon she will kill herself.

I've tried to get her to tell her parents but she flatly refuses. She comes from a family of eight and she was the favorite child. She says she can't let them down this way. Her family is against abortion.

Is there anything you can do to help? I would hate very much to lose this friend of mine, but I don't know what to do. I can't even talk to her anymore she is so worked-up and in such a nervous mess. There are times when she cries the whole evening and in her sleep at night. At times I think she is on the verge of losing her mind, but somehow she holds on. But how much longer? Please help me. She is like a sister to me. . . .

Dennis,

I decided to type you a letter cause I need some help on a problem that is really terrible.

Last June I met this boy, Eddie. He was 18 at the time and is 19 now. I'm 16. Well, we really had a deep relationship all summer. We were together every day and every night. I mean, he became my whole life. Pretty soon, he asked me to marry him. But he wanted me to run away with him and I was too scared to. But understand, I really loved him, it was just that I thought my parents would kill me! So then we both had a serious talk. He told me that if I got pregnant that would be a way we could get married. So I thought about it for awhile and then gave in. Well, it did turn out that I was pregnant, but it sure didn't turn out the way I wanted it.

Eddie knew that I was pregnant before my parents knew. But he didn't want me to tell them for awhile. So I waited as long as I could. But mom knew I was acting strange so she takes me to the doctor and finds out for herself that I was pregnant. She called him and he said that he would come up that night. I thought that we could just get married. But when he came up that night, he didn't give me any definite answer.

My mom had all my clothes packed when I came back that night and told me to get out, that I had disgraced the whole family. I didn't know what to do. The next night, I called Eddie and asked him to come up so we could talk it over again. Well, he was sick in bed so I went down to see him. Well anyway, when I went down there, he changed his mind about marriage and said that we were both too young. Why did he lie to me? I can't understand. When I found out, I wanted to die! I couldn't believe it. So when I came back home, mom asked what he said and I told her that he didn't want to marry me.

She told me she was taking me to New York that following weekend for an abortion. And that's exactly what she did. I really didn't want that but there wasn't anything else to do. But the very sad thing about it is that I am never allowed to see Eddie again! My mom went down to his house and told his mother that if she ever hears of us being together again that she would take him to court.

Now that's my problem . . . I call him every time I get the chance. I can't forget him, even though he did that to me. I cry often over him. What do you think I should do about it? Please help. . . .

Dear Dennis,

I am 18 years old and I just discovered that I am pregnant. My boyfriend doesn't want to marry me and I have no intentions of trying to force him into it.

We both agreed on my getting an abortion. One problem concerning the matter is that I'm not in too good health and I might bleed to death.

Abortion isn't legal in my state. I could go to New York over the holidays. I know a doctor who would perform the operation illegally. But he would charge me around $350.00. I could only get together $100.00.

I am just confused, I don't know what to do. . . .

Dennis,

Thank you for the fast reply to my letter. I am the girl who wrote to you because I thought I was pregnant. Well, at the time I wrote it was only 7 days after I had intercourse and I was worried. I desperately needed someone to talk to—even if only on paper. After writing to you my mind was at ease because I knew I was doing something about it. Since then I found out I wasn't pregnant, but rather my period was late. Thanks. . . .

Dear Den,

I am really happy to start out this letter with I *had* a problem. I hope you remember my call, but I understand if you don't. I called about a year ago, and as I look back on it now, I was on the verge of suicide. I was pregnant and very scared.

I didn't know where to turn. I heard how open and understanding you were and I called.

You gave me some of the best advice I've ever had. You told me to see a doctor, tell my parents and my boyfriend. It was a doctor who confirmed my pregnancy. As you said, my parents were really on me at the beginning, but I realize now how they were always there when we needed them. My boyfriend, now my husband, was really understanding. I was really surprised but then I fell in love even more. I was married on July 8th. I *know* that our marriage won't end in divorce. My baby, Michael, is well and happy.

Life is so good. I will try very hard to give so much back to it. If you turn to other people for support you can work through anything. Guess you know that. That's what you helped me believe when I needed it. . . .

As I talk with the girl against abortion, we explore the factors behind unwanted pregnancy. Her desire to debate shifts as she enters into the probe behind the complexity of people caught in this situation. I know that there are countless listeners facing the crisis of pregnancy. Eight or ten folks with this problem write every week. It has been a good rap. We have ventilated a number of feelings.

9:41—Host reads a letter from an unmarried girl who has been through an unwanted pregnancy and answers it on the air.

"Dear Mr. Benson,
. . . I went with this boy for over one year and during the last months I found myself pregnant. I told him repeatedly about the pregnancy and he told me to hold off till he got his job and a car so we could run away and get married. I did until the pregnancy started to show. Then I knew we

had to do something. He had a good job by then and a car. By this time I was 5 months.

His mother told him not to marry me. She said that it might not be his baby. Well, I can honestly say it was his child and that I didn't have intercourse with anyone else. The next month he had a new girl friend and came around where I lived and laughed when he saw me. He called me names to my friends and degraded me. There was no more he could do to hurt me. I thought of just ending my life and forgetting about the future. But I knew I had that life in me and that was something to live for. When I felt the child move I felt warmth and happiness, and I wanted to live even more than I ever did before.

My mother and I had a long talk and we decided the child should go up for adoption. But as time went on, I didn't think I could go through with it. As I lay on the delivery table and watched the child come forth I promised myself he would never leave my arms. I wanted to teach him how to love life and how to enjoy it, not like I did.

I had three long days to think over my promise and when I had seen the pain and sickness I had caused my mother I knew I had to make a final decision. Finally, I realized that the best I could give this child is my love and a home. But I was in a sick mind since he left me and I didn't know if I could do it myself. This child needed a father. My father has been dead over ten years and I know the value of having a father. So I decided the best for him was to give him up. It was the hardest thing in the world for me to do. Now I realize that it was the best thing for him. Through this ordeal I've grown up for a 17 year old girl.

My mother helped me all along and didn't turn me down or disown me like some mothers do. And now when I am in a lonely mood, I just have to look at her or be by her side and I feel loved more than ever and I live for every minute of my life.

Maybe some day this boy who deserted me will realize the wrong he has done and then he will be sorry. I can't say that I still love the boy because I don't. I can't say I like the boy cause I don't and I can't say I hate the boy cause I don't. I can only say time heals wounds and I know mine is beginning to heal. I have no feelings toward this boy and know somewhere, somehow and someway he will wake up to reality and see there are things he must do for himself.

I'd like to know your views on this ordeal. You have a strong mind and I really dig your program. I'll be waiting to hear from you. . . ."

"Wow! What a beautiful person! I hope that you are listening, sister, you have shared so much of yourself with us . . . What a nice head and spirit. I just can't help but believe that you are making something very nice with your life. . . . You will be strong because you are dealing with the real pain you have. . . . The last paragraph of your letter brings tears to my eyes. . . . You probably noticed that it was hard for me to read those lines concerning your feelings about the father of the child. With such honesty and sensitivity we will continue to have much strength. . . . The layers of pain and misfortune in your life seem to be recycled and internalized in such a way that you are wiser and more complete because of it. . . . I feel that you have enabled us to be close to you. . . . We care about you and thank you for enabling us to grow through the experience of your strength in the midst of pain and difficulty. Peace, sister."

"Wow! This is what *Rap Around* is all about. We are a community of sisters and brothers who care and share. No matter how bad your situation may be tonight you can overcome it if you reach out and accept the kind of help that is available in our community. . . . Call us. . . ."

It is hard to recover from the input of that letter and the call before it. People often kid me about my reverence for the language and thought rhythms of real people. There is nothing like the beauty of the written and spoken word from these *Rap Around* folk. It is stunning to absorb the insight and clarity of such self-expression. These same folks probably hate their English classes. I wish some classroom teachers could read the thousands of letters we have received. Autobiographical writing touches upon a primitive literary nature which many writing courses destroy. These encounters with folk writing and conversation leave me in awe of people. Even the most desperate person has so much to give to others. The process of human transaction (verbal, nonverbal) in the significant other relationship has a sacramental quality which projects meaning beyond the mere symbols of communication.

9:44—Fellow calls to talk about the trouble he is having with his boss. His employer objects to his grooming.

> "Dennis . . . I have this problem. I worked at a shoe store in downtown. Yesterday my boss told me to get my hair cut. . . ."
>
> "How do you feel about it?"
>
> "It makes me mad. . . . I have it styled and it looks good. I have been looking for someway out of it. . . ."
>
> "Your hair is important to you at that length?"
>
> "Yes, it is an expression of who I am. My long hair means something special. I can't really explain it. . . ."

"I have long hair and I can understand how you feel. . . . However, your boss does have the last word. . . . Perhaps, if you had a wig. . . ."

Dear Denny,

I am 15 years old (a boy) and a sophomore in high school. My father hates long hair. I started to grow it long. So he told me to either get a hair cut or leave the house. I left the house. A week after I left he talked me into coming back home. But he did not say a word about my hair. All of this happened about six months ago.

Just a few days ago a few of my friends came up to my house. The parents were out so I offered them a few drinks. Somewhere along the line my parents' whole bottle of whiskey was drunk or stolen. My father came home and saw the bottle was gone. Then he immediately rushed upstairs where I was sleeping. While I was asleep he got a pair of sissors and cut my hair! He completely ruined my hair. It looks so ugly because he cut out chunks of hair anywhere he could. My hair now has no kind of style and looks horrible.

What can I do about my hair? It's ruined and everybody will stare and laugh at me. Right now I am living at my grandparents' place.

I love my mother and father very much. I shouldn't have taken his booze. However, after what my father did to me I don't even want to look at him. Pretty soon I'm gonna have to go to school looking like this. Please give me some advice. . . .

Dear Denny,

About three months ago I shared a problem with you about my father cutting my hair, when I took his whiskey. Well, right now my hair looks alright and our family is back together again. So, I am trying to say thank you for the advice. It's great having a person who doesn't know who

you are or has never seen each other helping
people out. Thanks. . . .

**9:44—Girl calls to talk about sexual behavior. She is inter-
ested in being popular with the boys at school while
keeping her high standards.**

Dear Dennis,

(1) I really don't know how to go about telling
you my problem. It's not as big of a problem as
some kids have who call in on your show, but to
me it's a big problem.

(2) I have this problem. I'm a nice girl. I go
to church on Sunday and do volunteer work at
the hospital. I'm secretary of our youth groups
and belong to alot of clubs. I have alot of girl
friends.

(3) My problem is boys. What do I have to
do to get them interested in me? Should I go out
and get drunk and go to bed with every boy I
meet? It seems that's the only kind of girl boys
are interested in.

(4) If my staying a virgin means I'm going to
be an old maid the rest of my life, you better
believe I'm going to do something about that
real quick.

(5) I can't stand staying home alone on weekends any longer. It's driving me crazy always
going places alone. All my friends have steady
boyfriends and they wouldn't want me tagging
along with them whenever they are together.

(6) It's not that I'm ugly or fat. It's just that
the boys don't like girls who aren't high on drugs
or whores. If I have to live my life as an old maid,
I know I'll kill myself. I'm going to be graduating
this year and from the way things are going now
I can depend on it.

(7) My mother keeps telling me that when it
gets time for all those boys to settle down and
get married, they'll be looking for a girl like me

and not someone who ran around when she was young.

(8) I don't know. I'm all mixed up and confused. Since you are a man, you can tell me. Do boys really want the girl they marry to be a virgin or don't they really care? You probably won't know how to answer my letter, but thanks just for taking time to read it. . . .

Our kind of communication is built on such faint clues that we must use everything at hand to listen. When I get a letter like Patti's, a whole unconscious process begins to unfold. Even the envelope and stationery send out vibrations about the person. It may look like the Johnny Carson routine of fortune reading. However, so many things speak if we have ears to hear.

Patti's stationery is not like most letters in the pile of mail beside me. It is written on the kind of paper used in schools. Many letters come to us on some of the brightest possible paper. She has chosen to write with a pencil. One has to tilt the sheets at an angle to the light in order to make out the writing. There is a small peace sign drawn with a ball point pen in the right hand corner. It was probably added later. She must have reread the letter before she sent it. The envelope has been addressed with the same pen. There are a few erasures. This is not at all like most letters we get. Most folks just strike words. She has carefully composed it.

I wish that I could analyze handwriting. Perhaps this would make my work more helpful. Yet, there is a certain shyness reflected in the appearance of the note. She is reaching out, but with certain reservations.

The letter falls nicely into eight paragraphs. The opening is so much like most of our letters. It is a classic example of what counselors are taught when asked by a client where he or she should start. Just remain quiet. People will start where they think best. Patti also depreciates her problem in relationship to those of others. Yet, she is quick to affirm that it is very important to her. We are so often trained by our culture to make excuses for the sharing of feelings. It is thought bad form to unburden ourselves on others. She may also be questioning herself and giving me an out if there should be no answer to the letter. People really can't believe that they can write and really get a letter back. Even clergymen and youth workers express surprise when they write us and get a personal reply back.

Paragraph two of her letter is her presentation of herself to me. She nicely wraps up her life in limited space. All the outward signs of respectability and value actualization are here. She is busy in the right things with the right people. Patti is in the leadership pool with the comfortable position of secretary. The clubs she chose to name are accepted as "good" by the society.

The next block of input (3 & 4) presents the problem. She sets up the question and then immediately projects an unacceptable answer. It is implied that some girls get boys. Patti suggests that they get guys because of what she considers unacceptable behavior. She then threatens (herself, her mother, or me?) that she will give up her virginity if it can insure her of getting married. Does "old maid" really refer to marriage or is it just a metaphor for going steady? She is a senior. Some families put a lot of affirmation on girls who are clearly headed for marriage.

In paragraph six she fleshes out more about her feelings. She does feel isolated as far as dating goes. Patti apparently is experiencing the "left out" syndrome in terms of the social side of activities. She knocks down some possible reasons for her situation. It is not her appearance which keeps her back. Again, she attributes the success of other girls to their loose living. I feel a bit uncomfortable about this. Part of my own past is edging in here. It has to be sorted out. My high school days come flashing back. My value system ran along the lines of Patti's. It was no drinking, no smoking for me. Being in an aggressive male social pattern, I was able to date more than she has. Yet, there were parties on the beach where everyone was dead drunk, except Dennis. I used to drive my friends home afterwards.

Assuming the social role of a comedian, I was able to find a place in school activities and get attention. However, there were those deep moments of reflection when I knew that my popularity wasn't the same as the heavy dudes who told all those stories. I certainly didn't get that kind of response from the girls. Part of me wants to affirm her morality and yet part of me is suspicious that Patti is blaming the loose morality of others for her lack of popularity. This sounds like the relational game: "If it weren't for you . . ."

Paragraph (7) indicates that she isn't happy with her mother's position of deferred or eventual satisfaction. This "better later" advice never makes one feel very good at the time of crisis. At a later time the past won't seem so bad as it did at the present time. However, if you hurt now, you hurt. Has her mother accepted her argument about the reason for the popularity of others or has she planted it? I will run through her letter again. Have I missed anything which can help me respond to her? Paragraph six summarizes the lonely young adult's despair. At 17 she already accepts the coupling social structure and its exclusiveness. What powerful models of social interaction our society projects!

Perhaps Patti gathers her data for morality conclusions from the stories her girlfriends tell. She may be suffering from an acute case of the "pajama party tales." This is a version of "locker room conquests." Peers gather and fantasize about sexual conquests. The process adds some momentary entertainment and permanently makes reality much harder to take. I can still remember stories other guys told me about their sexual activities. I now know that they were exercising an age-old tradition of sexual my-thology. However, I can't quite forget some of these benchmarks as I look at my own life. Most people in such sessions secretly compare themselves to the persons in the tales they heard. It can be particularly hard for folk like Patti.

In the last paragraph she acknowledges her confusion. Here she does question her analysis about boys. Patti also understands that I am not really going to be able to "answer" her problem. It is interesting also that she justifies writing me because I am a man. Why doesn't she talk to her father? Maybe he is dead. However, it is amazing how many young women write to talk about sex because I am a man. They state that talking to their mothers and girlfriends is not the same as probing this topic with a male. Adolescent women seem to need males who are significant others. It is a shame that many fathers can't handle this kind of relationship.

As I handle this letter, I am beginning to get a feeling about Patti. I like her. She is trying to break out of the circle which now encompasses her desire to reach out.

Dear Patti,
   I have just spent a few minutes thinking about your letter and the concerns you shared with me. I had to relive similar kinds of experiences I had in high school. There is a difference. I thought at first that the girls only liked the guys who drank, did drugs, and were sexual playboys. These

were not my habits at the time. The first year in high school was hard. I was always on the outside edge of things.

It was the whole club and church group route for me. Yet, there was that empty feeling of being alone when everyone else seemed paired. You should have heard the stories my friends told me about some of the girls. It seemed that everyone was really swinging—except Dennis!

Well, there is no happy ending to my story. Nothing dramatic happened. Things did develop in a nice direction though. Somewhere along the way it became clear to me that I had to be who I was and that this wasn't going to keep me from having a great time. Then came the "life of the party" stage when I was the funniest (well, silliest) and craziest guy in school. Everyone noticed that I had fun without drinking. A few girls even dug my style.

A more important thing happened to me. I somehow discovered that everyone really needs care and concern. The biggest football star or the hottest chick in school yearned for someone to listen. Most of the kids in my school were dedicated to getting a guy or girl. If they couldn't make it in this way, they were ace students or jocks. Yet, there is broad popularity/friendship for someone who is genuinely interested in others.

The whole society seems to be focused on getting something or someone for selfish ends. When you turn this around, the tension which you now feel about your future companionship fades. While you listen, understand, and give of your personhood, you are being with other people. I will never forget one evening when a good high school friend (girl) of mine cried at my feet after a party. Her guy had just dumped her. I could love and care for her as a person. Later she helped me when I faced a similar situation.

Patti, I am going on too long. I dig you and your letter is important to me. You are a very sensitive person who has the capacity of looking into yourself and exploring the feelings inside. I am urging you to turn this gift inside out. Reach out to the boys and girls in your world and give them your concern. They *will* give their love and respect in return. Focus on others and others will discover those qualities which really turn another person on.

I don't know your feelings or understandings concerning the women's movement. However, listen to some of the things it calls you to be. You are not just a property waiting for someone to buy or reject. You are free to love and give in the exciting environment of today. There is no reason why you can't approach and befriend anyone. If you are seeking relationships in which care and concern can be exchanged, you have no reason to be hesitant.

Patti, my response to your letter is not asking you to wait. It is time now to start looking into the lives of others as a means of eventually establishing a relationship which might last a long time. Defy the games being played by others in school. Your gifts of who you are are needed by most guys right now. I get so many letters from guys who are afraid to speak to a girl. Who is there in your classes who never talks to girls much? You may appreciate his mind or comments. Yet, he is not one of the eight or nine "swingers" who have set the image for you.

It is good to be alive and free to be with each other. I know that you can break your introspective circle. Drop me a note and let me know how things are going with you. . . .

Dear Mr. Benson,

I have a problem. I am 17 years old (boy) in high school. I am much more mature than most other kids in my school. My mind is right and those who know me well know that I am a true "philosopher" at heart. I am interested in girls, not for the sex thing, but for the companionship and friendship. I want someone to talk with me personally and understand my problems.

My problem is getting this kind of girlfriend. There is one girl who is not going with anyone and is good looking, and I know she is an interesting person. I'm 5' 10" and weigh 200 lbs. I'm overweight by about 15 lbs. and my complexion could be better. (I'm not strikingly handsome, but I'm ok and trying to improve.)

Girls and boys first notice physical attraction and party kinds of behavior. I'm more of a philosopher and prophet than swinger. I can't just ask her to go somewhere because she may not be attracted and I wouldn't want to embarrass her and me.

This is driving me crazy. When I see her in the halls (passing by), what can I say without being aggressive? I am rather shy and I don't like to be plastic! I know you are busy, but please answer . . . just don't write the answer on a postcard. . . .

After finishing my letter to Patti and reading those of others there is a moment of reflection. A letter states and leads. It is not like a conversation. There is something so final and determined about it. I suspect that the fact that a response comes by letter is in itself a very positive thing. It seems to say that the writer has been taken seriously. It is easy to proclaim in a letter. I find that I cannot joke and kid the way the newspaper advice columnists do. It is a serious process to write out your problems and expose them to another.

One woman responded to my letter with a sentence by sentence commentary. She actually cut up my letter and taped the sections in her letter. It reminded me of the kind of reasoning used by a lawyer or a biblical interpreter. She wanted to know the precise meaning of language usage. It was an amazing ten-page document.

Another limiting factor in writing letters concerning problems is that the person often lives in a family setting. Apparently parents often open letters coming to their children. We offered to send our answers in a plain envelope. A letter coming from KQV would raise the interest of any father or mother. In most situations the letter usually has to be written without mentioning the original problem. This is particularly true when the writer has confessed the use of drugs or an unwanted pregnancy. The circumspect approach is difficult.

Sometimes the young person has a hard time getting the letter out of the house for mailing. Parents find notes and read them before they are sent or my answer before the addressee gets it. For instance, one fellow wrote about being a homosexual. I answered the note in as circumspect language as possible. I got an angry note from the mother of this boy. She said that she could see through my letter. She contended their son was not a homosexual and she would not give him my letter.

One week we received an envelope containing two letters. The note from the youth dealt with the girl he was dating. She had told him that she was pregnant and he was struggling with responsibilities of such a step. The letter was burned along the right margin. The second letter was from his mother.

> Brother Dennis,
> The letter from Marv got singed when I was trying to steam it open before mailing it for him. Makes me really sound like the kind of mother he seems to want you to think I am. But my motive

was to attempt to find out what's been bugging Marv, because he's been showing all the familiar traits that in the past have always precluded his running away from home. He has been miserable and I wanted to find out why so I could either help him or try to find someone who could. Maybe you'll be the one the Lord uses this time.

Marv didn't give you any background on himself, so if you do write him, please don't reveal that you know anymore than what is contained in his letter. He respects you. He's been telling me what a great show you have and I've listened to it with him, but you probably don't need any advice from me.

I agreed to let him drop out of school last year. Nothing would keep him there. He's very bright according to the school tests, but obviously too immature to use the brains he has. He works at a grocery store making $50.00 a week, but he has never held a job long because he is so resentful of authority figures and hates being told what to do by anyone.

This "chick" of his can tell him to do anything. She is older and aggressive. I suspect that this pregnancy story he told you is her invention and is probably not true. . . .

. . . *Please* don't let on you got this letter if you reply to him. God bless you and your program. . . .

We are committed to keeping the confidences of our folk. We have had to remove all the names and addresses from our files of letters. So many things are confessed in the epistles. The children of local political figures have written to us with a revealing picture of life in their families. Yet, there is another sense in which the writing of one's concern may be an unconscious attempt to tell someone in the home something. An English professor at the University of Michigan used to remind us when we were studying diaries and journals of famous writers that such efforts are really undertaken with the full knowledge that some day someone will be reading them. There are only a handful of our people who asked us not to read their letters on the air. The young man with the singed letter may have been inviting his mother to become a significant other by knowing that she would do what she did. However, that is between them. I wrote to them separately and did not acknowledge that I had heard from the mother.

In the midst of the rapid conversation with the girl about dating, Pat comes in with another Coke. He also gives a list of subjects waiting for me on the unaired phone calls. It is clear now why heavy calls must be conducted by me with the eyes shut. John is talking with a couple staff people in master control. They can be seen in the window. One part-time DJ is running around and carrying on in pantomime for four giggling girls who are looking through the window. I've got to focus on this girl's struggle with her morality and dating patterns. So many ideas and inputs keep washing through my head. Meandering thoughts keep poking up with each of her words. Other letters and other people wander through my subconscious as we talk. I guess all interaction is this way. However, there is so much stimulation pouring into me at this moment. News is just a few minutes away.

9:50—Boy calls in to discuss his recent religious experience and how his problems have been answered by this faith.

This call will trigger all kinds of reaction. This is one of the trickiest things to discuss. It is easy for me to slide into a communication manner which would exclude most of the audience. Being a significant other in a pluralistic environment is much more demanding than we suspect. For instance, the term we use for clergy so easily expresses our religious orientation. There is nothing wrong with your personal roots of faith. However, on the radio we want to have the conversation take on universal application so that many people can be included at some level. This caller has adopted the new language of his faith. He repeats the same clusters of words to describe his theology. It will be my job to push for definition. I will also want to test his belief to discover the breath of his experience. So many flashes and questions come to mind as the flow of recall concerning the varieties of religious experiences are stimulated by our rap.

> Dear Mr. Benson,
> I rejoice over the exciting new faith that I have. But it's more than just faith—it's *understanding*. It's something we all need—an answer to a question—any question. Then we can understand *why* this happened or *why* this is the way it is. The answer is there—all we have to do is understand it—and that takes time. It's more than faith and understanding—it's patience.
> It has been my dream ever since I *really* discovered Christ to tell my story—to tell how much Christ really does care. . . .
> There is such beauty and innocence in the story of those possessed by fresh faith! A new being with new language and a new outlook concerning everything. Can others really utilize the spectacles of faith and see their own lives differently through the experience of this new person? Or will elitism and zeal limit those who can celebrate another person's joy?

Dear Dennis,

　I suppose I should be consulting a preacher or a clergyman for my problem, but I feel much more at ease relating to you.

　You see I had a strong belief in God and practically nothing could question my faith. Since four years ago, when my parents separated and then later when we were back together again, I thanked God all along for the "miracle." Well, recently in science class my teacher has been challenging the Bible in terms of the creation story. The kids are starting to believe him. . . .

　Dennis, I wouldn't be writing to you if I didn't believe in you. I believe that you are a Christian just by listening to you. Please help me face the challenges raised by my teacher. . . .

What a difficult time a teacher has when he or she assumes the role of challenger. This person may be an intellectual bully or a perceptive mentor trying to get complacent students to think. Why are so few teachers cut from this cloth? Why doesn't the church educate the young (and old) believers to use intellectual as well as emotional equipment? Why can't the construction of a personal faith system be built upon the foundation of theological thinking? If emotion is the hook, when does the historical mentality come? Where can this young boy get support for the challenges he feels?

Dennis,

　I am thirteen and last summer I committed my life to Jesus Christ. It may sound surprising, but it was great for me! My problem is that it is very hard to be a "good" Christian. Some nights I've had a lot of homework and I don't read my Bible and pray. It gets harder and harder to get that "high" I had when I first accepted Jesus. . . .

Susie is undergoing the decompression process which comes when faith must be nurtured in isolation. Will this make her later faith more difficult because of the early peak and lack of developmental support? How does she deal with the feeling of guilt? Why so many highs and lows? Isn't there an emotional mid-range which can sustain faith and life? The whole society reenforces highs and lows. It is the media dope of Sunday afternoon football emotions or the daily soap opera catharsis all over again.

> Dear Den,
> . . . I feel when one prays to God he should pray from his own heart and not from what was in someone else's heart a couple thousand years ago. I don't believe in the way my father or the Rabbi makes me pray with the beginning about praise and going on through pleas for help and health. God knows what I'm thinking anyway. My dad or the Rabbi just walk away when I ask these questions. . . .

What are the languages of prayer? What is he really asking? Is it the adult dominated translation of the faith that he is resisting? Perhaps he just wants to be taken seriously.

> Dear Dennis,
> I'm fifteen years old and really into astrology and the black arts. At school, we often talk about astrology and everybody puts it down. They say it's a "bad thing" and I can not understand their reasons for thinking so.
> They all think that I belong to the witches' coven which we have in our community, but I don't. All this is only a hobby. I think that these things can really help us. How can I get it across to them that are the black arts is *not* a bad thing?

Why does she enjoy supporting that which others think

unpopular? Is this how the spirit which produced the pro-
test against the war and racism in the late 60s is now being
expressed? Is she using this interest to create an image?
Is this confrontation role her manner of coming into community?

Dear Dennis,
    . . . I am 17 and a junior in an all girls Catholic
high school. I have always been very much involved with church affairs. My mother went to
school with our pastor. I know all of the priests
personally. I attended an ordination of one of
my old friends. There I met Mike who was also
ordained and is now serving at my home parish.
We have become great friends and have serious
rap sessions at least once a week.
    During Christmas our relationship became even
closer. We went to a party and didn't get home
until 3:00 A.M. He kissed me several times, but
each was short. Mike is not the religious extremist
but goes out and does things most priests think
are against the old church.
    As a fact, I know he likes me very much. Each
day my feelings for him become more and more
personal. I was sent to him when he first came
because my parents and I weren't getting along.
He was very helpful. Each of us love to talk seriously and feel sex is not all that important to hold
a relationship together.
    The truth is that I love Mike very much. We've
never had any sexual relations, but have held
each other close and kissed innocently. The real
problem is his priesthood. He is a priest—forever.
He hasn't been a priest for even a year. Now he
is 24. I led him on. I can not just say "forget it."
It might sound like I am very moral and suddenly
I've had this downfall. Truthfully, I'd love to have
had other relations with him, but just keep thinking of that word—forever. It's strange but I'm

not worried about my own reputation—only his. No one knows about this.

I'm torn between him and what is right according to society or God. We can't go on living like this. . . .

Wow! Even if this is fantasy, it is dangerous. So many youth workers get trapped in this kind of dynamic. Most counselors are familiar with the transference stage of a client's development. It is harder with youth workers. The situation often calls for an "us (youth worker and students) against them (parents, supervisors, etc.)" unity. The youth advisor or young clergyman appears so much more human than the older staff in the eyes of youth. Innocent touching and affection can be misunderstood if the adult in the situation loses perspective. Some experienced workers who develop these kinds of relationships build in safeguards. One friend regularly discusses the relationships with a psychologist. This gives him some good advice for handling a relationship and an excellent way of checking his feelings. It is so tempting to drink up the love of your constituents. Many volunteers have to work on this. . . .

Dear Dennis,
. . . I go to a local church. All of the kids in the class come from different schools . . . to cut it short we can not get it together. It is very uncool for the kids (or so they think) to care about the Bible materials we are studying, who we are and what we feel. . . .

Adair is rehearsing the despair of organized religion. There are few contact points in local teaching situations which create community and excitement about the content. This may explain why it becomes quite easy for extra-parish religious movements to make headway. Personal care is the one factor a variety of religious movements share. This is why so many folks respond to a *Rap Around* model of programming. . . .

> Dear Dennis,
> . . . about 2½ years ago I started to go to a prayer meeting and in the beginning I liked them very much. We would all sit in a circle and talk about our problems and try to understand them. Then. we would sing, laugh and eat together. I guess you could call it one big party where people would come and try to understand themselves better through the help of God and other people. But then I just quit going because I felt I didn't have anything to give of myself and everyone else did. People would say things which confused me and I didn't understand. It just turned me off. But yet, I always wonder if I did the right thing by quitting. . . .

What was she giving and receiving from this interesting group? Have they sought her since her drop-out? The test of community is the second and third steps of concern. Follow-through is a major testing step in being significant to others. The pensioner who receives meals on wheels, the invalid being visited, the child in the foster home and anyone willing to receive the personhood of another needs assurance of a relationship continuing. In this case, Janet seems to blame herself. Why should she have to feel inferior?

> Dennis,
> . . . I can not resist the temptation to express my views on the boy who called about his spiritual experience. When you asked him about how this changed his view of the world, he put down the human issues that seem really important to me.
> I'm a Quaker and I would like to see this person come to a Quaker meeting and see the *love*

people can have for each other *and* for others in the world. We are concerned about peace in the world. During the demonstrations some of our people actually got between the police and demonstrators using their own bodies to keep people from getting hurt.

We believe in letting our love touch people in the world. This guy's heavenly and spiritual thing is nice. However, we have to let love out so that it comforts people. We do this for the sake of love and not to trick people into believing with us. . . .

It is strange how people dovetail into the comments of others. The fellow now on the phone with me will bring this girl's response. They are both right. Why do we have to fragment the directions of our concerns? There are those who volunteer and those who think good thoughts. It is sad when such personal inclinations keep people from appreciating the bit of truth which dwells in other people.

Dear Dennis,

I haven't written in so long and I wanted to drop you a letter now and let you know how I am. I'm really doing great. I've changed so much over the summer. I'm a completely different person now. My ideas have all changed and my attitudes about life.

I don't care about politics anymore and I'm out of drugs and that whole scene. I find now that my former life was so empty and unreal. My life was worth nothing—until I gave it over to Christ. I'm full time Christian now and I'm so happy. I found in Jesus everything I'd been searching for all my life—security, love, joy, understanding and peace of mind. . . .

It is good to see new life. However, I hope that Val won't have to disown her whole past. There was beauty and love in the old days also. She has dropped bad habits and hopefully is on the way to a bright future. Yet, continuity between yesterday and tomorrow is needed if we are to have stability in our lives. As George Orwell suggested in another context, we are not free if we lose our history. This is not to suggest a recital of the past should crowd out the present. It is good to see Val alive and happy again. . . .

9:54—Introduction to five-minute newscast.

4 A Long News Break

Mark Schaffer is now into the newscast. The trouble with the talk show's pace is that there are no real breaks. A DJ has that precious time while the records are playing. Lynn and Carolyn are at the station early. They are getting ready for the show which will follow after my next hour. They come into the studio and tell me that they have a *Rap Around* impersonation. Lynn takes my role and Carolyn is the caller.

> "Hello. *Rap Around.*"
> "Hi . . . I got this problem. . . ."
> "That is okay. Go ahead and tell me. . . ."
> "You see . . . no one likes me. . . ."
> "Yes . . . go on. . . ."
> "I am a bit overweight . . . I weigh 350 lbs. . . ."
> ". . . Heavy. . . ." (much laughter)

We laugh at my colleagues' parody. They are great talk show hosts. They have a finely honed sense of intellectual vigor. Pat brings in some messages from people who want calls after we are off the air. He reports that Joanne has come into the lobby and he talked with her. She is having a bad time at home again. She has returned to her perch outside the window.

The studio is cleared again. I punch the cue speaker for "on air" programming. The newscast can be heard. Mark is in the midst of a story from Ireland. ". . . was killed by a sniper's bullet. . . ." A sharp pain flashes across my mind. Two people float out of my imagination. Just two names, Catherine and Sean. Folks I have never met. Yet, two persons so very dear to me. I hurt from memories.

It seems just like yesterday when the envelope came in our mail bag. It was different from the others. It was simply addressed, MY BROTHER DENNIS. KQV. PITTSBURGH. The scrawl was bold and covered much of the small envelope. Its contents shook me to the quick. However, I could never realize when I read the letters what would transpire.

Sunday

My Brother Dennis,

Why I am I do not know and why I am free I cannot know, but I have killed and run away and I am free but I have found the peaceful religion here in your city.

I was born in Ireland and I learned always to hate the bloody English and the soldiers and the Proddys, so I worked hard last year for my people.

I was in prison but none of them could prove I killed the soldier so they let me go. My brother paid to send me here but I did kill the soldier and a little girl besides. I am sorry and I will never look at a gun again but I am afraid they will take me back to the prison and I want my brother to stop killing. I want all of them to stop.

I cannot be forgiven my sins for killing the child and the soldier. He was just a boy my age it looked. The child was like my little brother. Her hair was like his.

You are a kind man but you cannot understand. I am free and not free. *I am afraid.* I cannot pray to the Holy Mother anymore. I cannot take Mass. They took away my beads in prison and laughed and the priest said I couldn't have Mass and they laughed at my language and hit me and said they would kill me if I spoke Irish to them.

Tell them please in your city—killing is horrible. It is hell. It is hell. . . .

The following Sunday I answered it on the air. There had been no address nor would I ever get one from my new friends. I urged my brother to seek the means of grace that were open to him. I tried to affirm him and extend the care I felt for him. It was a one-way conversation. However, more mail would come. A moving and tragic love story would unfold that none of us could predict.

Dear Brother Dennis,

The last two weeks have brought to me a change. I feel as a human being again and that I do not need to run again. I cry in the night sometimes still but I am not ashamed. My Catherine brings me peace with the touch of her hand. She is gentle. She makes the past seem false. She stays my hand in anger. For her sake I will never be afraid again. I will take her to my homeland when I can and we will live there. She is not Catholic but she wills me to go back to church now my hand is still. I will do anything for her the Father says and I shall never be done. (A Gaelic prayer closes the note.)

Dear Mr. Benson,

I did not know that Sean had written you at all. He sets great store by you, and admires you, as someone who will not turn away anyone with even the slightest ridiculous problem.

There is nothing wrong with him that love couldn't solve. His parents taught him to hate exactly what you are (isn't it ironic?). With his friends his hate came out in violence and then he did what he did.

He found himself excommunicated, verbally abused, physically abused, mentally and culturally castrated and devoid of any friendship whatsoever. Having no other recourse, it seemed to him that he must hate himself.

When I first saw him, he looked as if he were in some sort of drug withdrawal. I found that that was not the case soon enough. What he needed the most was to talk with someone who would not abuse him.

He has scars and bruises still from the prison experience. He has decided with a lot of prodding to approach God again, through the confessional and a priest, as he believes. It was a triumph when he caught himself about to say "but I hate them all" and he didn't. He smiled, closed his eyes and said something in Irish that sounded like a prayer. For your sake, I asked him what the prayer meant that he had enclosed with his letter. It seemed hard for him to translate but, "I give, forever, my soul to Jesus Christ and pray for the Virgin Mary to witness this giving," was the idea of it.

Don't worry about Sean. He is strong enough to find his own way without me and without the church, but he doesn't know it. What he needs is love. He was strong enough to kill for his convictions (and strong enough to turn himself in), he endured the prison, his conscience, leaving home without a hope of returning and now he has hope. Thank you for listening. In Sean's interests, I won't sign, but I will write again.

Catherine called me after the show. She told me about her life as a nurse in the city. She and Sean were living together. She promised to continue writing.

Dear Mr. Benson,
I think perhaps a letter is the best way to speak to you. Sean is summoned to confession again.

The priest told me he's going to give Sean a hard time, because that's what he needs inside, a true knowledge that he has earned his forgiveness— really worked for it, and *"has gotten it all out of his system."* I can't personally believe that a man can dole out God's forgiveness in exchange for good works, but what counts is that he has cleared Sean's mind and who am I to say anything against that miracle?

It look as if there maybe light down the road concerning our legal problems. I can't fully understand it because of the many complexities.

We touched a moment in our phone conversation on the fact that we are of different religious backgrounds. That's putting it mildly! Within Christianity, we could not be more different. When we first got together, he tried out my faith. At first he was on to something, he thought, but it wasn't for him, he soon discovered. At least, he was inside my faith for a moment and he understands why I can't go with him into his with a whole heart. At least, we respect each other's faith and he'll never hate someone on the basis of religion alone again.

He nursed me when I stayed home from school, cooked, cleaned, sang and taught me Gaelic. He would have gone out and taken my nursing shift cheerfully if he could have. He must have mailed some of my letters to you.

If there is one thing to be learned from our experience—well, there's more than one thing obviously. War destroys. Love builds. Hate tears apart. Understanding mends. Peace comes from within. Seek and ye shall find.

We wrote to his sister and mother yesterday, and await a reply.

Dear Brother,

My dear girl writes a lot of letters to you. I found them and she says I can mail them to you.

Here they are. She had a hurt bad yesterday coming home but she will be good in a week, please God. I stayed home to take care of her and she is teaching me how to write right like a little child.

Do you see my letters are better. My dear is asleep now. She says Gaelic words in a funny way. She makes me laugh. She cannot chastise my English until she learns Irish perfectly.

Poor Catherine cannot walk or write and she looks very hurt, but she never says she is hurt. She is brave. And I hate to write like this. It takes too long but she says I have to.

Dear Brother Dennis,

Catherine is gone to work today again. She is the dearest soul in the world. God is good to us. We talked to her mother on the telephone again last night. She is good too. Good luck to you.

In her letter my mother sends her blessing to us all and to you, my new brother.

Dear Mr. Benson,

Sean is fine. The priest has him doing penance by working with children until he feels he has made up for the child's life and for the soldier's life he will pray. He prays with such an honesty and a belief that you know there is truly a God.

He love the little children at the school, they love him. He goes to church every day and sometimes I go with him. He has a distance to travel every day, but if he had to go to hell and back, he would walk it cheerfully. It is a pleasure to see his peace of mind. I never believed in a soul before, but it is so obvious his is being washed clean, by God's forgiveness or his own action, I do not know. I sincerely doubt his penance of prayer helps the soldier any, but it helps *him*, truly it does.

I have learned a lot from Sean. It has been

hard for him, hard for me. There will be harder times, I am afraid to say. He is in this country illegally and cannot stay here forever. If we delay, he may be arrested or deported.

Sean has the soul of a poet. He speaks English far better than he writes it. He has been reading a lot. His upbringing was in a country town. Irish was spoken at home and only enough English to satisfy the inspectors that English was being taught.

Thank you for being there, as the first person he turned to. His letter to you was the first step in his comeback from hate and fear. . . .

Dear Brother,

I am writing again, to send with my dear girl's letters. I do not know what she has written but I will tell you I am being freed. Have you ever stopped a little girl's cry and then heard her laugh? It is beautiful. I am permitted to teach a boy how to ride a bicycle and to tell them all stories I told my own sister once. When I must go I must. God will help. He brought me here to my dearest when I should have died. He will help us. God and the Blessed Virgin keep you. My love does not believe in her, but the Virgin blesses her the same.

PS: [in another hand] Mr. Benson, please note: I am beginning believe, I truly am!

Dear Mr. Benson,

Just how risky Sean's position is really struck me last night. If he should in anyway attract the attention of the police or anyone curious, he would have nothing to show for himself and he would be imprisoned or deported. I'm surprised he wasn't taken up for vagrancy sometime ago.

Outside interference is a worry that will be lessened when we go to my family home in another state, but if he should even get sick and have to go to the hospital (even the hospital where I work!), people would question who he was and his history. I wonder if he understands this pressure on him to keep out of trouble.

He isn't really free yet, but he feels free, and I don't think I could stand to dampen either his freedom, or his enthusiasm for going home. But for his own protection he has got to watch what he does and especially what he says. There is a false security for both of us. A legal friend says that we can't be too careful and it's a scary feeling.

The strange thing is, I draw my peace from him now, instead of the other way round. That is why it is a false security. We both stand on shaky ground and this manufactured confidence is a bubble which will break if either of us rocks the boat and or someone else sticks a pin in. Perhaps this will happen even if someone else breathes on it.

However, Sean's peace of mind and sense of self worth is the all important thing and we have achieved that.

If he were deported and re-imprisoned for the crimes he has paid for a million times over, everything he has achieved would be lost. We would be parted. I would have to go to prison for helping another human being. The fragile peace that seems so strong now would just snap like a twig. What we need is a true security.

At my home he can establish some sort of residency. It is the one bright light. I have confidence the right will come of it, out of this very real unreality. . . .

Dear Mr. Benson,

We must do something soon. Next month I go back home to another state. Sean will come with me, I hope. If he wants to strike out on his own, he will.

By the way, we have a new friend come to Sean's aid. I went to a fellow nurse's husband's friend who is a lawyer. He is a fine man and works for a great organization. I leveled with him about Sean, and he was horrified. Anyone who could kill a little child and a soldier, he thought— well, I don't want to relate his first opinion. I wanted him to know just what Sean was up against if he should be caught here. It's bad. It would kill Sean to see the inside of the prison again.

This lawyer is a good man. He decided to meet Sean before he passed any moral judgement. This man says he will give Sean any legal aid or advice he needs. Now Sean's got three friends and God bless everyone of you. There is you, the priest and the lawyer. You've respected our need for quiet, and most of all, you were there when Sean needed you.

The IRA itself is my main anxiety. Sean would not hold his tongue. He is outspoken by nature. His accent has already provoked questions once. If he should repeat to me what he has said in the privacy of home anywhere in Dublin, well, the nightmare—that he would be executed as a traitor. God, we both know it has happened before.

There is another nagging fear. We put our address in the letter to Sean's folks. If he should be wanted at the moment for something I don't know about, the authorities or the IRA could trace him through that letter. I wonder if they watch the families of runaways? I wonder if they intercept mail? That was stupid. Sean wants to know, badly of course, how his folks are. To let them know he is safe, or semi-safe at least. There maybe no problems, or it maybe the end.

You can see why we look forward to going to my family home. There is one neighbor within a mile of us. The nearest town is three miles. If my family can accept Sean, God they have to. We both have to go to work now. I'll write again. Sean, too.

Dear Brother Dennis,

My dear Catherine told me that she has told you of our plans. I am very happy. It is true that she will be married with me. I will go to her home now but she will come with me *in time* to my home and meet my dear ones.

Dear Mr. Benson,

I have news about Sean's folks, but I don't know how to take it. Sean isn't home yet. It is worrisome when Sean is not home on time.

Apparently, all is not well. The letter is from his mother. Both she and the sister are well, all the violence seems to be confined to the cities. She writes that Sean was on the wanted list until the direct-rule takeover by English Parliament, but since then no lists have been published.

A number of boys from his school were on the list and a number dead. A physical search was made in the town by a unit of paratroopers and two cousins taken away. She and the sister were questioned before our letter arrived and nothing has happened since then in the town.

Most disturbing, she writes that her husband in London was questioned and she writes that he suspects he was shadowed. My poor Sean. What kind of life did he lead? Did he ever believe in what he did? These questions hurt me very much. His face is like a mask. He will smile, perhaps breathe something in Irish when he reads the letter.

I remember his face of sheer terror. Now it is calm and hopeful. In his sleep sometimes the terror flits back. Once he cried out in his sleep. The nightmares he must have. But still it is all a mask.

I know this man. He is not a boy. He is a man,

twenty-four years old. We have sheltered together weeks that seem like months. If my mother
knew the situation, she would cry. She would point
an accusing finger and say—he's using you. He's
sleeping with you. And you have the nerve to
bring him here? I will admit to you as a minister
that we approached each other sexually once.
Then we stopped at the right moment. We both
understood. It was too sudden.

I feel as if both of us are afraid to admit we've
fallen in love. Is it love? Is it on his part an over-
reaction to his great need? On my part, a falling
for his mystique, and well, Irish handsomeness?
A reaction of our forced and, well, gentle intimacy in close quarters? A sort of over-extended
mother urge in me? He can't be independent
without a home of his own, and he can't have it
without the means and the indentity. I don't think
I'll ever know.

Love works in mysterious ways. Once I thought
I'd never fall in love. When I thought about it, it
was very different. My dream man would be
someone of my own religion, similar background,
secure and even wealthy. "He" would sweep me
off my feet and give me pretty things until I
finally murmured "yes", after "he" vowed he
would climb Everest for me.

What has God given me? A lean (and fatten-
ing up) frightened scarecrow, former murderer,
a Roman Catholic, exiled and unacknowledged,
even judged illegal, non-existant by the state.
What has God given him? A girl with nothing
but a place for him to live and care for him. For
sure, things he needs, but anyone could have done
for him.

Is there someone else in the world meant to
give him more than shelter? God knows, the man
has my heart. But are we misleading ourselves?
I'm waiting for an answer to come from some-

where. It will have to come from the both of us.
I love him, but have I got any right to? Only if
he loves me. I hear him coming up now. I'll put
the letter away.

Yes, I believe we are in love. Tonight we go
back to Sean's special priest to talk for awhile.
What will come of all this? Pray for us, please. . . .

Dear Mr. Benson,

Our time is so very near and there is so much
to do. Letters home and abroad are best written
now at 3 A.M. I can't sleep tonight. Sean is sleeping very quietly. I could reach over and touch
him, but it would wake him. I had to give him a
sleeping pill tonight.

Sean's father was shot while walking from the
ferryboat dock to a train station. It seems not to
have been accidental. There is no proof of whom
or why. The thought it might be retribution for
Sean's actions against the child make us sick. I
wish we would know if it were accidental or sheer
misunderstanding or mischief, but I suppose if it's
retaliation they'll let us know one way or another.
Sean is very quiet. I wonder if he is at all afraid
for the future? The condition of his father is not
critical. We are worried about this other thing.

Our lawyer friend has thrown up his hands in
frustration. There are so many snags. Our priest
friend can only marry us in God. I feel we are
already married in God. For Sean's sake, of
course, I will do the church thing.

I haven't seen my folks in ten years, but they
truly are anxious for us to get home. I left home
in tragic circumstances not easy to explain at the
age of 13. I will explain at the end of this letter.
I have resolved to. I want you to understand more
than anyone else what this homecoming means to
me. My home is beautiful. I don't know what the
years could have done to it, except made them
all ten years older and added 19 nieces and 28

nephews that weren't there before. It's a big family in a medium house. Even then, I have 10 brothers and 6 sisters. I was the 16th of 17 children all told. We had another brother, who drowned. Two little boys as well have died that way. That is a hazard of living on an island off the West Coast.

I will be so happy to go back with Sean. This idea of mixing another blood into ours is very queer. We are so inbred.

I have a poor fatherless daughter that will be Sean's child's sister. Sue was conceived in total horror and will be Sean's child in love. Our future children will either be sisters or sister and brother. One of my sisters has raised my girl like a mother, which I could not have been ten years ago. I've not seen her since her birth, but she's ten now. Old enough to understand?

To explain my daughter's birth is to explain, of course, why I left the island in the Pacific and went to see some of the world. I was thirteen then. I felt crowded then, and almost pushed out of the family. I liked to go wandering in the sand hills around home picking berries and sand flowers to take home. The child's father was 19 then. A neighbor, he wasn't right in the head. He had a rifle of his own and went shooting a lot on the hills and marshes between our houses. I saw him often, but at a distance. He must have seen me a couple times. I don't know. He hung around the edges of our clearing with his rifle. I didn't go out if I saw him near.

The day it happened I was going to a grass clearing pretty far from home that I liked especially. I was crossing the stream near it when he stood up behind the thorns on the bank with his rifle and said he would shoot me if I didn't go lie down on the grass. He played around a lot with mud and his knife. I passed out when he started to rape me. I woke up in the night with my muddy, torn dress covering me and his jacket.

There were lights distant and people calling. I ran home. They found him next morning on the marshes. When he saw them coming, he shot himself. He was clutching my sweater. I became pregnant and had the baby in a nearby mainland city. My sister took her home and I went into a religious home in Denver. They helped me go live abroad. When I came back to Denver, I was independent totally and an accredited nurse. I nursed a year there, then came here.

I accept everything that happened. It can't rule my life. It is no worse than Sean's story. The boy who raped me is dead. He was insane. He was very unhappy and he killed himself. That is all.

I wrote it out because I wanted you to understand what this homecoming means to me. I only wish it were Sean's home as well, because he needs a homecoming badly. It may become his home. I just don't know what. We leave this week. Please think of us sometime and pray for us. Love. . . .

Dear Mr. Benson,

Please be warned that I intend this to be a long letter! I think about you often now that I am home. Sean does as well.

We came down through mountains to the Coast. Then came familiar swamps at nightfall. Sean's first experience with a swamp. By moonlight it was utterly beautiful. After crossing the bridge, the road to home twists and turns, it is seldom paved and is hedged all around by tall thorns, vines and pines. That did not change in ten years. Actually, it seems nothing inanimate has changed.

Every light was on in the house and every man, woman, child and baby of the family was there. It was well past midnight, but they were all gathered and up. The poor house! There was music and food and a lot of children crying when we came up. The cross country trip has been so long that it was hard for us to time our arrival any better.

Poor Sean. He hadn't expected anything like the wedding he'd gotten, and he had it and he hadn't expected this family, or this welcome. Mother soaked poor Sean with her tears and Dad stood up (something he's never supposed to have been able to do now as long as I can remember) to greet him.

My daughter baked a cake for us. I cried myself for pride. It had kelly green icing and wild colorful ribbons of design. She looked at me like a little dog looks, asking to be patted on the head. She knows I'm her mother and likes Sean well enough. She's shy. When she gets to know us, she'll choose her home. We're living under the same roof now so there's not much choosing to do.

I told Sean about her in good time. Now I feel I should have told him long ago, but that's all passed. They spend time together. She calls him daddy now. The poor child has never understood exactly her begetting and why my sister's husband isn't really her father. I want her to feel for Sean as a father, of course, but I don't want her to be hurt when the truth gets to her.

She is not pretty. She looks a bit like her grandmother and a lot like the dead boy. I don't think her mind is normal in every respect. Disturbed child of a disturbed father and a child mother. Her life will not be an easy one. The three of us will have to make the best of it.

Sean has a paying job on a boat. My brother got the chance for him. It seems that Sean had experience on a fishing trawler when he was younger. This must be like a next-best-thing to homecoming for Sean. There are people who love him, an ocean, bay and boats.

100

We have no news of Sean's father yet. Our mail is quite slow. Sean's mother has our box office address, but it is ten miles away on the coast. Please, please do not think ill or be offended if I don't give you an address. I do trust you, and I know you wouldn't hurt us, but I asked Sean about it and he thinks it would be the best thing to continue to cover tracks. I'll write, as always, when there's something to write. We have always been anonymous. As long as we know we have your goodwill and prayers that is all we ask.

Before we left Pittsburgh you did a documentary on the film of Malcolm X. It was a good documentary on a good film. We both went to see it. I wanted Sean to know a bit about the race problem, to see a great black man on the screen before the attitudes in the country give him the wrong impression.

I went to see the mother and father of the boy who killed himself. They are very elderly and I don't believe in ten years they've gotten over their son's suicide. One of my sisters and her family are living with them now. Her family's income support these folks, as well as gives them a home with more space. The older people like having the kids around and have adopted them as their grandchildren. Sean, when he heard about this arrangement (it happens all the time) could not believe it. He studies it with the eye of a cultural anthropologist.

Our best to you.

Love, Catherine (and Sean in spirit. He's out with my brother now, trying to outwit a bunch of fish. I wish him luck.)

Friday

My Dear Brother Dennis,

I drew for you a picture of my new family. It is not over good. I am sorry but it is as good as I can do.

101

I am glad at work here. Still I do not feel so safe as Catherine hoped. I become more like an American. Yet, I am Irish and I do not want to forsake my motherland. I want to go home with my wife and Julie, my new daughter, to see my sister, my father and mother. I will go home. They can be so happy in the beauty of my home. When I look at her and the child, Julie, I think of home. It takes me long to write a letter. This one I am writing a few sentences a day. Most often I throw letters away. This one I will mail as before.

I must and will God give us rest. I have a fear in me. A fear I will be dead. I cannot explain why. Mater writes my father is coming better. I pray so. . . . (A drawing of three people enclosed.)

Dear Reverend Benson,

I do not know for sure if Catherine's sister did indeed get in touch with you. She was here last week to collect Catherine's things and gave me the packet to send to you.

Catherine is showing no sign of progress. I am very sorry to have to tell you. Her sister tells me she was very calm the duration of the day after the night of the murder, when she put her and Sean's things in order. The insanity came the night after and she had to be taken into the hospital.

There was never any hope of catching the murderer. Any attempt at that rests with poor Sean's parents.

The murderer knew of you and Sean's priest somehow. Your epithet was "the bloody radio priest." When Catherine's sister comes again with news, we will try to contact you. Thank you for your friendship.

Friends of Catherine's in happier times.

With this last anonymous note was enclosed a black bordered envelope. It simply read: "Please give to Dennis Benson, July 18." It was signed by Catherine's full name.

In the envelope I found Sean's small wood and silver crucifix.

It is so hard, very hard to catch the outside edge of human life. Being a significant other means tears and frustrations because so many times you can't intervene to help people you love.

John Yurek is frantically waving from the control room. My time warp of recollection has made my senses slip away. It is 10:00. I am sitting at the control board, facing the mike. The taped introduction has just about run its course. It is time to start the show again and I have tears running down my face. I must collect myself and get back to the phones. We have a full switchboard of calls waiting.

5 The Second Hour

10:01—Opening rap by host.

I am going to take a few minutes to set the tone of the show for the second hour. Perhaps a restatement of our thrust will help. We can't reenforce our kind of communication too much. An invitation to write letters should be made at some point. The process and time gap in getting answers back to the listener should be articulated. It is important to promise only that which we can deliver. There are so many experiences in which services and expectation cannot be fulfilled.

Rap Around and its people have nurtured certain feelings about what we are doing here and perhaps how it can be done. Our situation is unique. In fact, attempting to be significant to others in a public medium like radio has many disadvantages. There is a self-consciousness about the language which must be there. Being a federally licensed communication outlet means that we must maintain certain standards. For instance the call that starts out with the charge that a friend, identified by name, was the source of drugs is libelous and must be cut off. A few callers became so relaxed that we had a slip of language which had to be excluded.

104

Dear Den,

I wish you hadn't cut off that boy who called last week and said something you didn't want on the radio. I think that people should be relaxed in their conversation and should be allowed to say anything. . . .

The interesting thing is that several people I cut off the air called later and apologized about the use of things which were not allowed on the air. It was their contention that they were so relaxed that they talked to me just the way they would have in person. A significant other hopefully nurtures an environment where there is such comfort.

"Welcome back to our electronic community. *Rap Around* is the kind of place where people have an opportunity to be human and to be real. I think that this kind of community is important to the whole human spectrum. . . . When we gather around the cluster of feelings. When people celebrate the past it intrudes, and hopefully influences the present and maybe the future. How are we really going to be brothers and sisters in the tomorrow? How can we be brothers and sisters if there is a kind of churning inside and we haven't delineated the different dimensions: a gloomy portion here, the angry portion there, the fear, the happiness, the joy and all sorts of things come tumbling together? Perhaps we find ourselves doing things we don't mean to do to ourselves and to other people. Well, *Rap Around* is again this kind of experience where these things come out. If you want to be part of it, we suggest that you call us."

"Let's go to the phones."

10:02—Girl calls to talk about the problem of helping a dating rival overcome jealousy.

"How are you tonight?"

"OK. I met this boy at a party a couple weeks ago. It was at this girl's house. We became real friendly and everything. He drove me home. There was another party last week and we were talking. We were driving around and . . . making out . . . we weren't kissing or anything. We were just hugging. This girl who had the first party got really upset. Apparently she has a very bad crush on this kid."

"Wow . . ."

"I met her once before and it had been so messed up. I really tried to be friends with her because last time it was under such bad circumstances."

"Mmm."

"She got so fed up that she walked out on the party. Her feelings were really hurt and everything."

"Hmmm."

"Everybody in the youth group agrees that the girl is being very immature about it. It is just terrible. I don't want to hurt her feelings, but somehow she has to learn. She wasn't going steady with him. She has no claim on him. No real reason . . ."

"Hmmm."

". . . to act the way she did. I just don't know how to reach her. I would like to help her. Any suggestions?"

"You are telling me that there is a bit of jealousy involved here."

"More than a little bit."

"How do you break down jealousy? Let's say that she didn't have any reason to be jealous because of your relationship with the guy. If a person is into this jealousy thing, almost anything will provoke feelings. If you get behind jealousy, you find a lot of different factors. One factor maybe that the person has a lot of fear. Jealous folk are afraid not only of losing the thing or person, but that they are going to lose their security. As you dig further you may find that a jealous person may have a lot of hostility to dump out. So you are dealing with a very common, very strong, kind of emotional reservoir. Have you talked with her?"

"I haven't talked with her at all."

"I don't know how mature you are. She will likely jump on you when you call, but I would try to call her. . . ."

"I tried to call her. She is out of town."

"I would take the initiative. This is what a mature person does. Confront her with sensitivity and talk it through with her. If she comes back at you, try to keep from becoming defensive. She will say some explosive and perhaps unjust things and then you will respond. . . ."

"It really doesn't bother me so much that she is acting this way. It is going to hurt her later on. When she gets to nineteen or twenty and starts acting this way, she is not going to get anywhere. She is going to need so much help."

"Why don't you start the process? Reach out and try to talk with her and see what happens. Keep your head in the right place. Pick up not just what her mouth says, but also what she is feeling. You will be surprised what can happen."

"I am probably the wrong person to try and help her because of the boy. If it weren't for that, it would probably be a good talk. Everybody is really upset and mad at her because of the way she acted. I may be the last person to help her out."

"I have found that sometimes the people who

explode the loudest are the people who are not sure about themselves."

"*I am sure that this kid has her share of problems.*"

"That's a good point. Maybe you can't help her. You are not a psychologist. I am just urging you to try and if you can't . . . move on. You are the best one because you are the one, in her mind, who has pinpointed the whole thing. You carry more power even though it is a negative thing than anyone does. . . . Also keep yourself from bad mouthing her with other kids. I have found that if you can say something nice about a person while being honest, it will get back to that person. We often live up to what people expect of us. I try not to bad rap anybody . . . I slip a lot. . . . Hearing positive things said about yourself really helps to heal wounds. You can help her by having your friends forget it too. You seem to care."

"*I try.*"

"Good for you. Good luck. Let me know how it goes. Peace."

10:04—Call from man who is newly divorced. He is confused and bitter.

"*I am having a problem. My wife and I have just gotten a divorce. It has been hard. My family and her family have been down on us. They don't want nothing to do with either one of us. I think that this is a pretty bad thing.*"

"Did your parents play any role in your marriage? It sounds like they are quite active now."

"*Oh yes. Quite definitely. My mother especially. . . . She is the type that noses into everything. She isn't happy unless she has something to do with her family to make things a little bit more to her thinking.*"

"Hmm."

"You know what her point of view is? If anything breaks out in the family, she has always got to be there in order to give a helping hand. And in the first place it was my mother who forced the marriage between myself and my wife . . . my previous wife. She had made her seem like such an off beat woman . . . There were a few things I had done before we got married . . . We have four children. . . ."

"How do the children reestablish a new life?"

"The children should not be without a father or should not be without a mother, right? Everybody feels this way. But why should a child have to watch his father or mother fighting all the time? What kind of thing does this do to a child? I have seen this myself. My mother and father didn't get along too well. I was afraid to bring my buddies home all the time for fear that my dad would be in a bad mood . . . yelling and screaming at anybody. He might tell them how bad this was or that was. It is not only me. I have seen this with other people also. I have seen it with other families. My wife . . . my former wife had the same experience as friends of mine who come from families that were stuck together just because of the children. Their whole lives were ruined as well as the lives of the children. I don't believe that this is something that should be."

"What are you going to do about your present situation?"

"I don't know. I am in shock now. I guess I am looking for someone or something to blame."

"Have you had some counseling help?"

"Yes. But it is hard to go through this treatment."

"Hang in there with your counselor. I am impressed by your willingness to push at your situation with such honesty."

"*It took a lot of guts to go to that head shrinker. But, it does help.*"

"Keep in touch. I care about what you are facing. Let me know how it goes. Peace."

"*Thanks, Dennis.*

Dennis,

I am a 22 year old male with a problem that is soon going to drive me insane if I can't pull through it soon. I was married at age 18 to a lovely girl who was only 16. At that time we were in love very much and did not have to get married. After 2 years of what I thought was a happy marriage, she finally walked out on me. Her reason was that she met another guy who she loved more than me.

As a result, I got the "I don't care attitude" and started taking dope. After a few bad trips, I finally was able to quit the junk, although I was still left with no one to turn to.

Now I have had three friends of mine killed in Vietnam, a few married, some in college, and the rest are either engaged or going steady.

I can't seem to get another girl friend since I was married. When I am able to get a date they don't seem to dig me because if they don't already know of my problem, they seem to sense it because of my actions. Some girls find out from people who know me that I am divorced and that ends it real fast. They think it's my fault.

I feel so disgusted anymore because of this lonesome life. I just don't even feel like living at times.

I'm laid off from work and don't even have enough money to go to places where I could possibly meet someone.

Dennis, I need someone to turn to or at least

some friends to be with. I can't stand this lone-liness much longer.

I'm not a very good letter writer, so if you can't understand anything, please mention it and I will write back. Thank you for your time. Peace!

Dear Mr. Benson,

I have a serious problem that I would like your help on. I am 23 and I have a little boy. My son's father and I were together for 2 years before we broke up. We broke up in July and since we broke up I have met another guy. He is married, and has 3 children. But what worries me so is that he says he loves me very much and we've only known each other for one month. He's always asking me if I do love him and my answer to him is yes. But to be honest with you, I really don't love him at all.

I do care a little for him and that's all. But since we've been dating, my son's father has come back into my life. He used to do a lot of drinking and that was our reason for breaking up when we did. We have talked about going back together. But I really don't know if I should do this or not, even though he says that he won't drink anymore. But I still don't know if I should take him up on this or not.

I still care for him but I just don't know what I should do about him or this other guy that I am presently dating.

Would you please help me with my problem because it really has me in a spin and I really don't know which way to turn, so please help me because I would appreciate your view point very much. May God bless you with peace. . . .

Dear Mr. Benson,

What you are about to read maybe the saddest letter you have yet received. I was married at 19 years of age because I was carrying someone's

111

child. At the time I loved this young man very much. Well, we told our parents and we knew how much we hurt them.

My parents didn't want me to marry but I thought it was best. I knew I broke one rule so I wanted a huge wedding, knowing it was wrong my parents gave me one anyway. The night I was married I was three months and knew that I didn't want to get married but did anyway. All my former boyfriends came to the wedding. It made me sad that I was getting married.

Mr. Benson, I want my cake, ice-cream, and eat-it to. In other words, I'm miserable with married life and being tied-down. I have a seven month baby girl. My husband isn't what I expected him to be. He is two different people. He loves me truly, but I don't love him. I want my freedom once again. Just to be able to do what I want on my own.

I want you to know Mr. Benson that I'm no tramp. I come from a wealthy family. We lived in a big beautiful home. So you see Mr. Benson I don't come from a low class family.

I no longer want to be married nor do I want the responsibility of my baby. I have a career waiting and that is in modeling. . . .

Dear Dennis,

I have this problem. It's about me and my brother-in-law. I am in love with him. We have had an affair. My sister found out about it because he told her. He had told me that he was in love with me. This has been going on for about a year. We planned on getting married. He told me that he wanted to get a divorce. I slipped out to see him whenever I could. I couldn't go on hurting my sister anymore.

I am still in love with him, but I've finally come to my senses that he was only hurting me. If he really loves me, he would leave and we would run off and get married. I haven't seen him for a few weeks. I can't live without him. I'm always thinking about him. I can't seem to get him off my mind. I don't want my sister or her children to be hurt again and the same with me. He is 31 years old and I am 18. I'm all mixed up. Please help me. . . .

10:07—Host reads of complaint from listener concerning the handling of the show.

"Let me share a letter with you. We have so many calls on *Rap Around* that they back up. So this means that people cannot usually talk about someone who has just called. Everyone who is on the line has something on his or her mind. I got one letter from a sister who corresponds regularly with me. It is kind of important to me. I want to take this opportunity to share this letter."

Dear Dennis,

I listened to your show last Sunday. At about 11:30 a person called in about a bird. I think that she was disguising her voice. She was putting you on. I think that you handled it all wrong. I would have said . . . then she has an expression I can't read over the air . . . and hang up. Don't you understand that people know how you are and that they can call you and make a fool out of you?

They know that you will take it because all you ever talk about is love, peace, brother, and sister. I don't understand you. What is it that won't make you get mad or angry or scream? Why don't you try sometime . . . she has a series of exclamation points and question marks. . . . I thought I knew you through your letters. I don't have to meet you in person because you express yourself quite clearly in your letters.

You *were* . . . the word is underlined . . . one of the few people I thought highly of until last night.

I guess that I had you all wrong. It is not that that little incident is so wrong but I think that it shows that you must handle bigger situations the same way. . . . Then in really large letters she continues . . . . You have got to put some people down. Believe me it won't kill them. When you give advice, you always stick in: don't put them down, show them that you care. Well, what if you don't care? You can't handle everything with love. You are fooling yourself and it just won't work. . . .

"I am going to respond to this letter in detail by mail. However, let me make some comments about it here. I think that it is good to reenforce something. As you know from *Rap Around*, we reach probably 40,000-60,000 people. The rating figures indicate that this is the size of the audience listening at this moment. We are very happy about such an audience. We also know that our audience is composed of people from different age groups. I get letters from grandmothers and people much older than the ten-year-old who might call. We are a community in very happy, normal situations. Some of these folks write about how great life is. We have other people who are . . . very . . . discouraged. They are people filled with despair. There are those very sick. Some folks are in great need. Perhaps these two hours on the radio mean a great deal to someone very lonely.

"The whole purpose of *Rap Around* is not really my advice because I am not wiser than anyone else. *Rap Around* tries to care. Laura, I am sorry. I can only be who I am. In some situations I do get angry and mad. But I don't feel that *Rap Around* is such an occasion. *Rap Around* is a love affair. It is some place where I don't feel angry.

"I am not unaware. It is true that some people

call us who are not too together. They think that they are putting me on. But I am not going to take the chance of putting them down in return. Because they might be in an emotional situation tonight where this is the only way they can communicate. There are some people so confused that all they can do is shout out. On *Rap Around* people don't have to shout or make a noise. They can talk and be heard. I try to care for them and treat them like persons of worth and respect. If I were to put down someone who was merely testing me to see if I really did care and I shut them off, I could never forgive myself.

"This show is important to me. I suspect that it is this treatment of love which is reflected in such a beautiful audience. Laura, I have offered my life at one point for what I believed. I have used confrontation when the occasion called for it. I have marched against racism and the war. If I have the courage to do that, I can certainly use my sensitivity to listen to *Rap Around* people as you mention.

"Laura, I care about you. I hope that my act of love has not damaged our relationship. I can accept those who do not feel love at this point . . . without any judgment. We have to be both who we are and who we are becoming. . . . Peace, sister."

10:09—A young man (17) calls to talk about a friend who is into drugs.

"I have this problem, Dennis. I have this friend who is an acid freak. I am straight myself. I have been trying to talk him out of it for a long time because I know that it can really mess you up. He disagrees with me. I have shown him articles. It really shakes me up. Because whenever I am with him, he tries to talk me into it. Everytime

*I have a harder and harder time resisting this
reasoning. I don't want to break off with this kid.
He is here with me now. He wants to give his
part of the story too. Can I put him on?"*

"Sure. Put him on . . . (sound of phone changing hands). How is it going, man?"

*"Well . . . you see I am this kid's friend. I
am just experimenting a little bit. I am not trying
to find myself or nothing . . . I, I, I never lost
myself. We have a little problem. I don't want
to haul him down. I don't want to bring him
down with me, you know."*

"Hmmm."

*"But . . . we are pretty close friends. We go
out and have a good time. He doesn't want to
make the scene. I don't want to bring him down.
But he keeps trying to pull me out of it. I want
to do my own thing. I just want to groove a little
bit. Everybody likes a little bit of adventure, a
little bit of action, you know."*

"But isn't it important to you that your friend
really cares about you? He is not a bleeding heart.
He is simply a guy who likes you well enough to
be concerned. He is not like your parents who
are on your back as a matter of their role. He is
a friend. And yet, he says that he is concerned
about you. Whether he is right or not isn't important. What he is risking to say to you is an
act of friendship. That is really important."

*"I see that. That's why I don't want to have
any hassles with them. Ya . . . I don't want to
bring him down. I don't pull him down, but I get
sort of radical when I get into something. I
dropped a couple tabs of acid recently. I really
dig it. I really enjoy it. I am not saying that
everybody should try it."*

"What I hear you saying is that you should respect him for what he is into. You folks should

116

be able to remain friends and yet be in your own worlds concerning this matter. I have a lot of friends, but they aren't going to force me to do everything they are doing and I am not going to force them into what I am doing. Yet, we can make it together as friends. I hope that you are saying that your friendship is important enough that you can respect him and you don't have to force him to do your thing. I am sure that you aren't dropping acid all the time. So there are other times you can do the things that you both groove on. It sounds as if you do have mutual respect."

"I do respect him. But I can't see why he is always coming up to me and calling me an acid head. He keeps showing me all these articles. I dig, you know. I read them and that, you know. But I am doing my thing and he is doing his, you know. I can't see the point of him trying to change me. He started out with the "look here" approach. He is now getting real radical and saying that I am out of my mind. He says that my kids are going to come looking weird. Do you have any percentages on chromosome damage?"

"No. I can understand how you feel about this pressure. If we were to have some time together to rap about this I certainly wouldn't show some tables on how many people are damaged. That's not the point. For me, the whole drug thing—pills or drinking—is really a symptom of something else. If you have more fun on acid than living. . . . Wow! Your life must be quite down. . . ."

"Ya, where we live there isn't too much going on. I am bored."

"Ya. If you had to describe me, I am a media freak. I just spent the whole night putting together a sound collage. That blows my mind. I am standing at a tape machine for twelve hours.

With a headset on, my head is in the clouds. It is far out . . . there are no drugs at all. I just have to turn on life. Music scrambles my brain. I am high all the time."

"I dig what you are saying. I would like to get into something like that where I could get my mind off my boredom. If I could do something I really enjoyed, I would take on to it. I really don't like drugs that much. But I haven't found anything better yet."

"I dig what you are saying. I have a lot of friends who are fifteen or sixteen years old who are doing media with me . . . doing radio and television shows. We get into some really exciting stuff. It really blows our minds. You mix together all this stuff and out comes something new you have created . . . and it's dynamite. I think that you are right about the dullness of so many kids' lives. Hang together with your friend, brother. I think that he cares. I think that you both have something to say to each other. Maybe he should get off your back."

"One more thing, Dennis. I would like to get into some more raps like this. Is there anywhere I can go to get in a discussion like this?"

"How old are you."

"I am 17."

"There is a great new place downtown. . . . I am partial to my friends . . . Norm, who runs it, is a close friend of mine. He is going to have a place where you rap like this. It is called "The Whale's Tale." He is a good guy."

"You mean that he cares."

"Yes."

"I'll look him up, this was good talking with you. Thanks."

"Keep in touch, brother. Peace."

As I talked with this fellow, I flashed on all the similar raps I had had off the air.

There is a strange linkage of credibility which occurs once you have demonstrated your willingness to be a significant other. When people experience the process of your concern, they tend to grant you more ability to help than is possible. It is just the opposite extreme from the status of most institutions. People who hear you being a significant other know that you can help them.

It always un-nerved me to have people approach me in public and launch into a problem without an introduction. I might be eating a hamburger in a drive-in when suddenly somebody sits down beside me and says in a nervous whisper, "I think that I got V.D. Where can I get help?"

One evening after the show the old car refused to leave the parking lot. The next day a tow truck finally agreed to deliver it to my friendly garage near our home. The driver of the truck was very talkative as he hooked up the wounded vehicle. "It's the transmission. It will probably cost you a hundred and a half. What do you do downtown?" I told Bruce that I did the show on Sunday evenings.

> "I listen to the show. I think that you are a phony. You can't really care about those crazy people."

"I try to care about them, Bruce."

> "Do you really answer those letters and things?"

"Ya . . . I get to meet some of the folks."

> "I am not used to people doing things without a hitch. Hey, do you mind if we make a detour along the way? My dad is going to have heart surgery tomorrow."

We pulled up in front of the busy city hospital. The tow

119

truck with our car in tandem was left in front of the hospital. He put the huge flashing parking lights on.

"Hey man, would you like to go up and see him? I think that you might be able to help him. He is pretty uptight about tomorrow morning's operation."

We visited his father and after a few minutes we were back on the road. This kind of thing often happens when you rehearse our kind of communication in a public arena. Instead of using trust to sell people toothpaste or breakfast food, we can use pre-accepted care to enable people to be helped.

There is also a private dimension to this public exchange of personhood. There was one listener who sent many letters. He was very lonely and extremely talented. He was one of the best listener poets I have ever read. His poetry was written in two languages. Jerry was a homosexual who was struggling to hold on to his life. He claimed that my voice and human concern became a major focus of his love and poetry.

One week I read a particularly sensitive poem he had written. It was so good that it had to be shared. His next letter was confused and angry. He claimed that the poetry had been just for me. I was quickly forgiven and sent a twenty-page collection of his best poetry. He requested that this material never be shown to anyone but my wife. This material was written as the voice of his heart. It was only for me. I have never shown the material to anyone.

Poor Jerry was locked into a vise which kept squeezing him. If you could only have allowed others to share in this sensitive probing! He took his life a few months later. A creative and loving spirit was lost.

10:12—Girl calls to talk about friends who don't approve of her boyfriend.

"I have this problem. I am going with a boy and all my friends are laughing at him."

"Why?"

"He is not very cute. But I really like him."

"What is the problem?"

"They make fun of me concerning him."

"That is the decision you have to make. If someone is important to you, you stand by them."

"But these are good friends."

"Are you saying that their opinions are more important than your view of him?"

"Well . . . What they think is important to me."

"There are times in life when the opinions of our peers . . . friends of our age . . . can be the most important value. That is okay, however, a time must come when as a mature woman, you will make decisions about people in terms of who they are . . . not according to what someone else thinks. . . . I have found that someone will always laugh at another's friend no matter how handsome or beautiful that person may be."

"They may just be jealous."

"That's possible. The reasons for their approval or disapproval may not be very good."

"I guess that I have to think about this. I like him . . . and I like my friends. This could probably happen sometime if my folks didn't like a friend that I had. Thanks for your time, Dennis."

"Peace."

Dennis,

I have a problem that maybe you could help

me with. I have a girlfriend who is a really nice girl. She does smoke and all that stuff but she really isn't bad.

She doesn't have a mother. Her mother died when she was in the 4th grade. That's why I think she acts sort of weird sometimes. My parents used to let me hang around with her but now they won't anymore because she smokes and goes barefoot and stuff like that. The weird part about it is, so do I.

I always hang around with her in school and whenever else I can. We are really good friends. But whenever she asks me if I can go anywhere after school I have to say no because I'm not allowed. I can't just tell her my parents won't let me hang around with her anymore.

My mom won't even let me have her in the house or let me talk to her on the phone. Her dad just remarried so now she has a step-mother. My girlfriend keeps calling and my mom tells her I'm not here. She's really nice and I like her and want her for a friend but I can't.

How can I be friends with her when my parents think she's a tramp when she's not? Thank you for your time . . . I hope that your show is on for a long, long time.

10:14—A black woman calls to talk about interracial marriage.

"Dennis, last week this girl called to talk about dating a black man."

"Yes."

"I just wanted to say that I am a black woman myself and I don't believe in those kinds of relationships myself."

"Why?"

"For one thing it would be sort of hard to go with someone from a different race. You have

to work so hard to be sure that you loved each other."

"This should be true for every love relationship. Love is hard. One has to work at it in any setting."

"It would seem that this relationship wouldn't last. I have heard in a lot of racial relationships that they don't last very long because of the way society is. It would be very hard to have any kind of permanence at all. Society looks down on you for anything different. You see interracial couples walking down the street and everyone is looking at them. If you look closely, you can tell that they are uneasy themselves. They can't even have any kind of comfort in the relationship. I believe that if I am going to have a relationship with a person, I am going to be at ease with him at every possible time. If I am walking down the street with someone and everybody is looking, I couldn't relax. If I were the kind of person who didn't care what people thought, that kind of relationship would be okay. I think that most people in the world do care what others think. If you are going to be uneasy, why go through all that? I feel when the relationship matures and they have a child, the child will have an identity problem. They are not going to know whether to go to white people or black people. I think that is too much to put on the child. They are going to have enough troubles without the additional race question. In this kind of society you have to belong to one or the other because there is so much racial distrust. If the society were different, I would say that it is fine. But the society isn't that way. At least, not in the United States. If it were just going to be you and the other person, it would be okay. But you have to put all those problems on the child."

"Do you have personal feelings about marrying a white person?"

"[laughter] . . . I just can't see how a person of one race could love anyone of the other race. The world has conditioned you to have certain feelings about people of the other race. The white people have stereotypes about the blacks. And the black people have stereotypes about the whites . . . I am no different. . . . If you are to love a white person, you still believe some of the things that the black society has told about them."

"What do you say to those who have already fallen in love? It does happen that people meet and fall in love. It is not an academic question. It concerns people. If they have worked through the questions seriously, I can just bless them and affirm them."

"Yes, but the whole society isn't that way. You are one of the rare people."

"It is hard to make it as a young couple. Every couple has to face certain trials. In-laws often are critical of the mate. . . ."

"Yes, but this extra burden makes it even harder. Why put all these extra things on the relationship?"

"In the future there will, hopefully, be some change. Even now people are mixing more and will fall in love. There is a degree of love which is irrational."

"Ya, but the irrational love usually doesn't last."

"Ya, I know . . ."

"I am saying that if you know yourself that it might not last, then you should avoid it."

"I believe that you have to balance the romantic with the rational. I am glad that the irrational aspect of love is still there. It helps us get through the rough spots. It has been good talking with you, sister."

"*Later.*"

"Peace."

Dear Dennis,

About a month ago a family moved out of a house a couple doors down from us and across the street. Several families looked at the house, so far about three people have been interested in buying it. The reason for this was they were asking too much for it.

About two Saturdays ago a colored family looked at the house and showed real interest in it. The reason I'm writing is because of my parents. After the colored people left my father went over and talked with the real estate man to find out if they were going to buy. He said they probably would because they really liked it and they could easily afford it. My father also found out that their general income was higher than ours.

The first thing he did was to get an estimate on how much we could sell *our* house for. I asked him if it was because of the Negro family and he said yes. I felt really ashamed for him and my mother to because she shared his feelings. I've tried to talk to them but they just lecture me on human property values.

I was embarrassed *for* them because they were too insensitive to be embarrassed themselves. Other people in the neighborhood are acting the same as they are.

Three days ago a white family bought the house. Now their problem is over. It's the principle involved. They really didn't care about hurt feelings or anything but their own prejudices.

Many other kids I know feel the same way as my parents. I really feel sorry for those people.

I just wish black and white could live together. I'm 13 years old so anything I can say to my parents really doesn't have much meaning to them. . . ."

Dear Dennis,
   I want to thank you for helping me the last time I wrote. If you remember, you told me to let you know how it goes. Well, I think all is going great. I really dig my new brothers and mother. Sometimes people look and think something like, "there goes that girl who has black brothers and a black mother." But, it doesn't bother me. It used to bring me down but I'm sort of proud that I can live with colored people and not fight. Not many people really can. . . .

Dear Dennis,
   There is this boy who calls me every night without fail. He's asked me out a lot of times and I've run out of excuses of why I can't go with him. He said he'd do anything for me. He said he feels toward me as he does to his sister.
   The point is—he's black and I'm white. My mother and father don't know. They are very prejudiced. They ask me about him and ask me why I never invite him over. I like him very much. He's really nice, but why can't he understand that it will never work? I'd like for us to be friends, but if I say anything to him about it, he'll get hurt. I don't want to hurt him. Please tell me how I can let him off easy without hurting him. . . .

Dear Dennis,
   I'm so frustrated. I'm a senior girl in high school and I hate the kids so much. I really hate high school. Did you like high school?
   Anyway, there's this problem with the black kids. They are such rude and vulgar people. Honestly, they have no respect for teachers or anyone. At pep assembly they make noise while

126

the coach is talking. And it's *all* of them. There were just some white kids doing it.

This is my problem. There's this one black kid who constantly cuts me down. Everytime he sees me he embarrasses me in front of all my friends. I can't take it anymore. My dad says I shouldn't say anything to those blacks. I'm getting an ulcer. . . .

Dear Den,

. . . I go to an intermediate school which is very large. My problem is at school there are both coloreds and whites. Some of the coloreds have threatened the whites to cut their hair if it's long. A lot of the girls got scared and got their hair cut. I don't think that's right. . . .

Dear Dennis,

Recently my pal, Sam wrote to you about me. You replied and I thought that it was indeed a very relevant point you and he had. Let me tell you although Sam is white and I am black, it doesn't matter because I believe strongly that "a man that's a man is a man." No racial prejudice should ever be brought against him. Some people think this relationship cannot and will not work out but Sam and I know it will. We can face this without any type of embarrassment or whatever because we have guts and we like to set a good example for other people.

Well, my point is that one of my brothers thinks that this friend of mine should be my enemy, but I will not give in. He's really getting on my nerves and so are some brothers and sisters in school. It spreads you know. But I'm a man and I won't give in even if they call me Uncle Tom. Sam won't give in if they call him Uncle Ben. Your support gives me confidence. I need it. . . .

Dear Denny,

My sister is 18. She is planning on moving

away from home very soon and living with a black man and his brother. (My family is white). She has had intercourse with him. She has been lucky enough not to have a baby. Right now she isn't too sure.

My sister tells me everything and tells me not to tell my mother. I don't want to tell on her but how can I tell sister to slow down before she has a baby? If she has a colored baby I don't know about my parents. . . .

Dennis,

I got this problem. Me and my friends really like black people. We aren't prejudice. We think of blacks as people. We like black music better than white music.

The real problem is our brothers. They are prejudice and they are always jagging us and calling us "soul." My brother always tells us that we make them sick and that we are probably going out and marry a black guy. But we aren't. We're just not prejudice. What should I do? Blacks never did anything to them. But they still say they are no good. My brother thinks that they are no good blacks except these two that he knows real well. . . .

Dear Denise,

I got a super big problem and I want your advice or help. Our school is going to merge with a school that has a number of black kids. Now, I was going with this kid from the other school for almost nine months. While I was going steady with him, I met mostly all of the negroes at that school. The girls in our room are sort of prejudiced against the negroes. There is this one girl, especially, who never quites. She said that when the negroes come up, they'll tear the place down and there will be nothing but fighting in the halls.

I defend the black kids. I told them that I met most of them and that they're really nice people. I tried to reason with them, but it just isn't any good. It is disgusting as well as heart-breaking. They call these good kids by such terrible names. It hurts really bad to know just how much hate and prejudice there is in some people. I'm trying so hard to make them see that they are wrong. . . .

The interplay of ideas and feelings from other people burdens the person assuming the significant other role. However, the degree of involvement is such that one doesn't become the other person's emotions. Pat and I have talked about the many problems people are willing to share with us. Do you take them home with you? Do you lose sleep over the letters you receive? Not really, well, not usually. This doesn't mean that you don't care or that you shut people out of your mind. There is an amazing pool of strength given as you give to others. This reservoir of love and care enables the significant other to absorb people and feelings without being drained. There are tears, anger, and frustrations. These attributes of living are present in the lives of all those who love. Our kind of communication is just the external actualization of that which is usually reserved for a narrow range of relationships. The style of life which demands continual emptying of self for others replaces the giving energies many times over.

One of the strange side attributes of this style of relationship is that a whole new perspective of human nature emerges. The social tracking of cultural training which forces us to judge people on limited data is derailed. One understands more completely the solid rock of his or her values while becoming free to permit people to be who they are. You can experience opinions and life styles which are totally alien to yours without the anxiety over wanting to fight down what you are hearing. The bite and vigor of people caught in the process of becoming is hopeful and affirming.

10:18—A 13-year-old girl calls to complain about her treatment at the hands of a girlfriend.

"I have this problem with my girlfriend."

"Mmm."

"See, like . . . she has this thing against me. . . ."

"What do you mean?"

"Well, she has this servant-master attitude . . . with me. This one time I got mad at her and I said, 'just stop treating me that way.' She asked me, 'how do you mean?' My mom said to me, you know how mom's are. They think that their kid is the greatest kid."

"Hmmm."

"And she said to me, 'why don't you break off with her?' But she has been my best friend for years."

"How did your friend respond when you told her about the treatment you have been getting from her?"

"I told her that . . . it seems like she was sort of mean and then she . . . didn't understand. Or she acted like that. Do you know, you get on the street and sometimes you get whistles. She takes out a brush and she starts to do her hair and acts all big and all that. Well, she seems conceited a bit."

"You have given me an example, but why do you think that she acts conceited? Let's get into her head. Why does she want this attention?"

"Well, her mother . . . her mother, she was

*like ill and she was in the hospital. My friend
had to take care of herself on her own, she had
to shift for herself, you know?"*

"Hmmm."

"And maybe that is why. . . ."

"What you are telling me then is that since
she has had to go on her own she might be a bit
insecure. Now we are not to play psychologist.
But, let's say that if you pick some of the feelings
behind her behavior so that you can have a relationship based on being persons and not master/
slave."

*"She gets mad at me. She is sensitive. We
went down to the shopping center, you know.
When I want to go she will say that she doesn't
want to go. Sometimes she will break down and
go. So, like yesterday she says to me, 'do you
want to go down to the shopping center with
me?' I said that I just wanted to relax because
I went down to the shopping center all the rest
of the week with her. She started complaining
about it. I told her that I won't go down to the
shopping center with her. There was no reason
to get mad. I just didn't want to go."*

"This sounds as if this is really important to
you. You sound very sensitive about this too. How
do you continue the relationship and at the same
time maintain your self-respect? Have you tried
to talk this out calmly? You mentioned an out-
burst once."

"She gets mad when I try to bring it up."

"Wow! I can only encourage you to develop
some means of communicating on this at a deeper
level. Perhaps you can talk about feelings when
you are not in a bad situation or a disagreement.
Keep in mind the things about her past which
you mentioned. Her needs for attention and a

servant are indicators of who she is. Yet, you have the right to be treated like a person. You are not a doormat."

"Some of the girls at school told her that she had really changed. She is a certain age and she acts like she is twenty years old."

"How old is she?"

"Thirteen. They say that she acts like she is a queen or something. That really hurt her. I mean . . . I didn't think she would care, but then she started to cry and get all upset."

"She is really sensitive . . . you also seem sensitive. Hang in there and keep trying to communicate with her. Peace."

"Thank you."

10:21—A woman calls to talk about her boyfriend who is in the local prison. She uses the show to encourage him. He listens from his cell.

Dear Dennis,

I was married in 1967 to a girl of 18, I was 23 at the time. She was what might be called a mama's girl and wasn't quite ready to leave home. We have been separated since 1968.

I have been locked up since April, 1969 for arson. My wife has written and asked me for a divorce several times. I answered and told her to go ahead and get it, because we could never get along anyway. She has not written within the last three years. I have written to her a number of times since, but received no answers. My problem is I would like to know the way I can get a divorce from her. It would have to be under a pauper's oath, because I only make $7.00 a month. Thanks. . . .

Mr. Benson,

I have only been here in prison for a short time.

I have listened to your program every Sunday. I like it and I think it's wonderful for the kids to have someone to pour out their problems to, and to try to help them in whatever way you can.

These problems may seem very small and trivial to their parents to be bothered with, but believe me they are a very real and honest problem to a teenager. Especially important are problems involving sex. A teenager will consult a stranger for advice before he or she may go to their parents. This could be dangerous because with the wrong advice a teenager can and will turn away from a normal society if given the wrong advice. I know what I'm saying. I've already been through it. I didn't have anyone that I could really turn to for advice, and the ones that should have helped me as a teenager were the ones that did me the most harm.

Keep up what you are doing as long as you can. Teenagers need you, or someone like you, if there are any more around who are willing to listen to kids, but not treat them as kids. . . .

Brother Dennis,

I just finished listening to your program and felt I just had to write. The young sister (17) who called, concerning her 21 year old boy friend who is a drug addict and fugitive.

My situation is (or was) almost identical although I am thirty and my woman twenty, I feel I can identify with them. Believe me when I say what he is attempting is not cool in no way.

A junkie cannot survive, especially while trying to run and hide. It is impossible to support a drug habit without getting into something illegal.

This sister must realize that every junkie needs help, but unless he sincerely wants it, all the help in the world is useless. I had been a heroin addict for years, I also tried shooting everything and I thought drugs were really cool.

I had been in various drug programs, in the hospital often, in fact, even pronounced dead of an overdose, but that didn't bother me. In fact, nothing did, until my woman gave me a choice— her or the spike. Believe me this really hit hard. I knew if I lost her I lost my life, and I had no life at all with dope, so I took her.

When I was arrested I was still a fugitive but not a junkie. I am to be released soon, and she has kept her word, she comes to see me every week and is still waiting to marry me. She has not let me down and I know I could *never* let her down now.

So brother, if she really wants to help her man first she must make him be a man, and I know a junkie cannot be a man in any respect. The dudes here agree you are doing a good job. Keep helping the young people, before they are here writing letters. . . .

Dear Dennis,

I try to listen to your program every Sunday. I find it very interesting and very nice of you for being so nice to people with problems.

I have a million problems, but I will just give you a few of them.

I guess one of the main reasons I am writing you is so I can get some mail, and maybe you can give me some kind of encouragement. I need it. I am just about ready to throw the towel in.

I am charged with an infamous crime and the administration of the institution they put me in always keeps me up tight.

I am in the prison on what used to be "death row." I haven't been convicted yet. I have been in jail over a year fighting the charges. I was twenty-three when I was arrested . . . now I am twenty-five. I feel at least fifty. I am charged with five counts of first degree murder. I also have over twenty felony indictments pending against me.

I am getting awful tired of fighting. Since I have been in here, I have lost just about everyone I love. My family or relatives won't even write me and my wife is divorcing me. I can understand my wife because she has had a lot of pressure put on her by the police. But I can't understand everyone else. I don't think my personality could be that bad. When I was on the streets, I had all kinds of friends. It looks to me like everyone could have waited at least until I'm convicted.

To tell you the truth I don't even care if I get convicted or not. I have no place to go if I do get found not guilty. I feel so useless.

I don't even have anyone to write to because they don't want to be bothered. You know Dennis, I have spent over a year locked in one very small cell and . . . well, a lot of other treatment. As much as I hate to admit it, I have even broken down and cried. I just want someone to care. It is hard to explain. I have no one to talk to. I guess some people have it worse.

Dennis, because of what I am charged with, people seem to think I have no feelings. They don't think that maybe I am innocent. Everyone thinks I am guilty and that is it. No questions!

It's really a heavy case. I sure needed someone to stand by me until it was over. But it has lasted so long, everyone has given up on me. I sure need a friend.

You know what really gets me uptight? I have three younger brothers in trouble. One is in a reform school and the other is in the jail back home. The remaining one is headed for trouble. My parents live about ten miles from the county jail and they won't even go to visit him. My dad won't even sign the release papers for one of them to get out. That really hurts me.

It just hurts me so bad that it makes me weak-minded. I almost pushed the panic button. There are five boys and two girls in our family and my sisters and three of my brothers have been sent to reform school.

I don't care what happens to me, but when I see one of my small brothers getting hurt like that, it makes me wish I could just go insane and forget I know anyone so it won't hurt so much.

Well, Dennis, I will let you go because I am running out of paper. I usually write stuff like this to myself to try and ease my mind. You know, writing all my problems on a piece of paper. I just hope they let this out because I sure need someone to talk to. . . .

Dear Denny,

I'm one of many inmates here at prison that doesn't have anyone to communicate with and I'm very lonely. It seems as though I am a forgotten soul behind prison walls. If there are any good people out there in the world so close but yet so far away, please write me. . . .

Dennis,

I call you by your first name and realize first name calling should be reserved until after introductions have been made and a reasonable amount of time has passed, but we listen (especially those of us who are fathers) to you every Sunday since your program was born.

Your program has given me some insight of what's happening with the kids out there in the free world. I urged my children, two boys—15 and 18, and a girl 19 years old to listen to your program. They think it's out of sight too!

To give you a brief run-down of my present situation. I'm doing life and 30 to 50 years. I am charged and sentenced with killing a guy in a hold-up. I've been here ten years. In all that time, my daughter proving to be the most devoted, has visited and corresponded more than anyone else. Perhaps, that is one of the many reasons I love her so.

My heart actually hurts for those poor, little innocent, people after being introduced into narcotics. Hang in there!

Hi,

Well, brother. I got the grand-daddy of all problems. Well, let me give you some facts first. I'm 24 years old and I'm serving a life sentence for murder. That's a problem in itself, but here's my headache. I have a wife who is 22 and a little girl who is 2 years old. Now I'm trying to get myself used to the idea that my wife will have to leave sooner or later. But man like it's really getting to me. She is forced to live on welfare and we both know that's no way to raise a daughter. My wife is young and I know she needs love and, of course, the baby needs a father. With the kind of sentence I've got, it is almost impossible for me to be out before 15 years. I know it's not right for me to expect her to wait that long for me. I've told her I won't beg her to stay and I won't ask her to leave, that when the time comes she'll have to leave on her own. I mean I'm really trying to get myself together, and face this like a man but, wow, it's blowing my mind. I listen to your program every Sunday and I really dig how you come across. But is there anything you can tell me to help me get myself together? Please help me if you can!

Dear Mr. Benson,

I am writing a few lines to commend you on your show and what it has done and I sincerely hope it will continue to help the people especially the young people whose families don't have or take the time to help the youth. I must say that I truly believe that some of the residents at this prison wouldn't be here if they had someone to talk to when talking could have been quite helpful. Dennis, I can safely say that over 50% of the residents listen to your program. . . .

We received many poems from prisoners. There is much creative talent residing in penal institutions. In the whole society there is a real need for those who will be appreciative recipients of other people's becoming talent. Most people don't have time for those unpolished in their skills. Many musicians can only play for themselves. There is no outlet. We are surrounded by closet poets who can't or are afraid to publish their work.

> Dear Dennis,
> Please, I want to know what you think of this ignorant piece of literature. I wrote it because I felt it and I thought it was okay because I never can seem to find words to express my own thoughts or dreams, nor do I feel safe revealing them. However, at this moment I feel like letting or asking you to read this and see what you think. . . .

Rap Around often featured such works of art. We developed segments in which poetry was read. Some of the most confused persons could harness their energies so beautifully in prose or poetry. Some people would send forty or fifty pages of their verse. The subjects of their writing were amazing in range. Poetry can be an excellent way of working through frustrations and crisis. It is exciting to rap with a person around the occasion of a poem. We have had moving sessions when a person would read a poem or short story written months ago. As we recaptured the emotional state of the person at the time of the writing and related it to the present, a sense of movement or development could be acknowledged. The author could sometimes see for the first time things about his or her life that had been missed at the time of the writing.

One brother wrote to say that he had been writing

songs for the past few months. He was a college dropout and just spent his days and nights writing music in the attic of his parents' home. He was filled with creativity without any place to share these gifts.

After several letters he sent a tape of some songs. Finally, Jeff agreed to come on the show and share his music. We played a few songs and rapped about creativity and the human feelings behind this kind of probing. When we last corresponded he sent me several short stories. They are good. He plans to reenter college and his head seems to be more together than has been the case in the past.

His *Rap Around* appearance was his only public display of his music. Many of the literary pieces he has shared with me have not been seen by anyone else. I have enjoyed him and his art. He has also found someone who affirmed this extension of his personhood. Those in quest of being a significant other will find the realm of the arts as one of the most exciting dimensions of relationships. There are so many creative people in quest of listeners.

Our relationship with prisoners through *Rap Around* has been most heartening. The mail part of this communication became very regular. We were always impressed by the concern they had that younger people should have opportunity to talk with someone. They could identify with a person needing help at some point in his or her life. There was much more tolerance for the needs of others than among others. The seventeen- or eighteen-year-old young person would be tempted to radically disassociate himself from the very problems he or she had experienced two years ago. The tendency among so many of our *Rap Around* folk was to devaluate previous problems of themselves as they currently affected others and over-value their present problem. Perhaps this is the nature of human creatures. However, the significant other must be keyed to a level of pain and concern no matter what the objective rating of the problem might be.

> Dear Dennis,
> Just discovered "you" and *Rap Around*. At first I became a little irked—as you talked with children so long. Then you told me off in your little talk about how we should care for the hurts of others. Thanks. I needed that! I should realize that an eleven year old should be listened to. . . .

We also received a lot of communications from prison families. All kinds of difficulties about the prison situation were pointed out. Russell Martz, then public affairs director of the station, and I spent a day at the prison. Russ became actively involved in the publication of a controversial prison paper. We had the run of the prison and I was able to tape a number of interviews with prisoners. I could then share the insights and concerns of these folks who couldn't call with our wider *Rap Around* community.

The role of the significant other seems particularly applicable to the prisoner. We would get letters from very hardened criminals who were crying out for a caring person. The use of mail could be utilized to great advantage in this case. So many of the men never received any mail. The significant other is freed from judging those who have been tried and are now being punished for crime. Imagine how this application of being significant to others could utilize folks who are handicapped or limited in mobility! There is a whole range of possibilities suggested by the needs of prisoners.

10:24—Young man calls to talk about a problem he is having with his steady girl.

> *"I have this problem. I am going with this girl for five years, you know . . ."*

"How old are you folks?"

"I am nineteen and she is nineteen. The only thing I ever got off her . . . was like we are friends, you know . . ."

"Do you go with her to get something off her or do you go with her because you like her?"

"I mean . . . ah . . ."

"Does she like you?"

"Yes."

"Do you like her?"

"Ya . . ."

"What does she say?"

"We talk about it occasionally. She is scared, you know, she is scared something is going to happen."

"Do you think she is wrong to be frightened?"

"In a way. But I don't want to necessarily go all the way."

"You just want a different pattern of affection than you currently have now?"

"Right."

"That is a serious question. I get a lot of letters from girls who wonder what guys are all about. Many of them have the impression that fellows just want to use them. Perhaps she is indicating that you really haven't proven that you really care about her as a person. You are also raising the question of what courtship is. I can't really answer that. You two have to talk this out. You better work it through now because as long as you feel slighted and she feels unsure about your love there will be trouble on the path. Perhaps it might be helpful to talk to someone about this. Give me a call after the show and I will put you in touch with a counselor friend who has helped a lot of couples work out things before they get married or make a deeper commitment to each other. Good talking with you, brother. Peace."

141

The response to this call will be heavy. It will come mostly through the mail. It seems that the adult-young person communication concerning sexuality is strangely stunted. In the course of our kind of communication this realm will be touched. Sexual concerns are always difficult for the significant other. It is hard because many significant adults are not sure about this area of concern. They may not be sure about facts in many cases. They are often not sure how they really feel about sexuality. Of course, just about everyone is living a certain consistent value pattern which defines his or her sexual behavior. However, such modes of actualization don't promise that we really know what we feel about sexuality and sexual behavior. The growth of sexual fantasy literature is a good indication of this secret realm of feelings in many people. Perhaps there is nothing wrong with the fact that many live out a sexual life style different from that in the recesses of fantasy. However, it is extremely easy to project the tension between these realms in our minds upon the person seeking to work some patterns in his or her life.

The significant other must again struggle with the internal conflict which can arise in these situations. It is okay to have the sexuality values that seem important to us. However, our thrust with another is to enable that person to become according to his or her capabilities. We enable the other to work at the struggle. It is unfair to make them fight our battle or accept the conclusions of our lives. Some counselors or directors of youth might define their roles as including the persuasion of the client. However, we are not nurturing that side of the significant other relationship.

Dear Dennis,
I have been going steady with George for 6 months. I'm 17 and so is he. Before I started

going out with him, he had never gone out with a girl before. He is shy, but I don't really understand why he never went out before. He is good looking and has a great personality. I have gone out before, but not a whole lot.

I love him a lot and I hope that someday we might get married. We will both be going away to college in the fall. I told him that we should break up. I did this because he needs more experience dating.

He has changed a lot since I've been going with him. It took him 3 months before he touched me, and 4 months before he kissed me. Now he's not shy at all. I love him very much and that's why I'm doing this. . . .

Dear Mr. Benson,

I'm 16 and I've only had one boyfriend. My problem is that I don't know how to kiss! That's it in plain, simple, words. The first time Jon (my boyfriend) tried to kiss me, on the lips, my reflex was to turn away. Since then he has tried very hard to kiss me, but I turn away every time because I'm afraid. I don't know how to kiss him. I do, very much, want to kiss him only how?

Dear Dennis Benson,

I have a problem and I really need your advice as a *male*. The problem is affection. It seems that with some boys I can't make myself show a lot of affection. . . .

. . . I went with this boy for several months. We kissed but never really actually made-out. So this one night, he started doing these long kisses and I really couldn't stand it. He asked me what was the matter. So then we started to talk about why I was so dead. I told him that it wasn't all me and it was his fault too. Well, he couldn't accept that.

Well, he stopped dating me because I didn't kiss right. Dennis, how do boys want you to be?

Most boys say their girls aren't affectionate enough. What do they mean?

Dear Dennis,

I have a question to ask you. Do you think it is wrong to make love to your boyfriend? I am eighteen years old and go with a guy who is a junior at a local college. I have known him for about four years.

Just recently he moved into an apartment. That's when we started having sexual relations. I really love him and he feels the same way. I just can't talk to my parents about it. Like they really trust us as far as letting us go away for the summer together. Also I really love my parents and wouldn't want to hurt them. I would like your opinion on this.

Dear Den,

I'm 17 years old and have been going with a guy for a year and a half. We love each other very much and are planning to get married when I get out of school. He's twenty. We have sexual play, but. We haven't had intercourse, although it's getting harder to avoid it.

We want to express our love to each other so bad, but . . . we're scared of the outcome. We realize the trouble we could get into, but we wouldn't want to get married under these circumstances. We don't want to hurt our parents either. I think that's why we've refrained from it. Can you get into trouble the first time you have intercourse? How can you prevent trouble?

Dear Mr. Benson,

I hate my father. We fight all the time. Last year I went to Florida. I got a crush on one of my teachers. The problem was that she was also a girl, and I'm a girl. So, it seems to me that a girl getting a crush on a girl is weird, but it happened. When I came home at my father's insistance, I was miserable for months.

144

After that I kept getting crushes on girls. I am now 16 and still get these crushes. During the summer I got a crush on this lady whom I have known all of my life. I am now filled with feelings of love for my English teacher. She listens to all my problems.

I feel so much like a homosexual when these things happen and it takes so long to get over the hurt from losing these women. Could you tell me if you think that I am a homosexual or not? It is very important to me. Maybe I just act this way because of the trouble with my step-father. . . .

Dear Dennis,

I am a 17 year old girl and although this may sound like a put-on, I am not the least bit interested in sex. I enjoy male company and I've even gone steady. I don't see what's so exciting about an hour long necking session. I would get most vibes by talking with a guy!

Most guys I've dated say the same thing, that I'm just frigid and that I should see a shrink. What do you think? How can I overcome any guilt feelings when I kiss a guy, etc. . . .

Dear Mr. Benson,

I am a girl of 17, who met this boy 20 at a party last January. He would call me and we would go to various places and do things together.

Well, one night he explained to me how much he really loved me, how I was different from all the other girls, and he asked me to go steady. I told him that I felt I couldn't accept his ring because I wouldn't allow myself to be tied down. He went along with me, but it seemed everytime we were together he would complain how much of a drag I was because I wouldn't go along with his sexual wants and desires.

As it turned out, he began seeing another girl

who satisfied his sexual desires. But he would still want to be with me. It was like he had me as his good-image girl and would see the other one for some fun.

At first, it didn't matter to him, but as time passed he felt our relationship wasn't complete unless I gave in to him. He saw the whole thing as this being only natural and that everyone else did it, so why not us.

There are times, when he stops by to see me, and he'll tell me how things are and what he's been doing. It hurts me to see him like this, because then I begin to look back and remember all the good times we had together.

I just hope that he finds something good in life and will be happy. I'm sorry that I couldn't give in to him by the way I was.

Dear Denise,

I'm going with this boy who is in college and I really love him. We're planning on getting engaged next summer. About three years ago I was in a very different situation. I was walking around a park and a couple guys surrounded me. I didn't give in to any of them, but they all ganged upon me and overpowered me.

I am afraid that my boyfriend will find out and I will lose him. No guy wants a girl who has been raped. I feel so guilty about what happened in my past. I really had bad times after this happened and I just can't get this guilty feeling out of me. I really love this guy I'm going with and I really want to marry him. . . .

Dear Dennis,

I am now divorced and have one daughter. I am expecting a baby in September. I was assulted, raped, attacked, or whatever the word is. I planned to have an abortion, but I changed my mind at the last minute. I just couldn't do it.

I am planning on moving at the end of March. We are going down south to live. This is the problem. My family. As soon as they find out, they will be all over me with a million questions. Who? What? When? Where? How? My step-father said he knew I wasn't no good. Why can't people see I've done my suffering and will continue to do so for a long time?

Why is society the way it is? Always condemning others. I know it's no fun time having 2 kids and no husband. Don't people know that hardships and hard times are punishment enough for anybody?

Dennis,

I am 16. There's a real big problem—I'm a little worried about telling you all this but you're the only one I can trust besides God! I do need advice.

There's an older man I know. He's 42 and the father of five kids. I'm good friends with the whole family and I go to school with his son. I also work at the recreation center he has. I'm very mature for my age and we got into a little discussion one night and I guess you could say he took advantage of me when he drove me home. He keeps telling me when you're growing up your body needs things. Is there something wrong because I have this sudden desire? It's just a mood I get into once in awhile. He can't say anything about it or he'd go to jail. No, all he did was caress me from the waist up.

The following night I went to where he was and he asked me to do something that scared me very much! So I haven't been going near him or the family since. But the part that scared me was I would have done what he wanted me to if I knew how, but I didn't. That's terrible! What's wrong with me?

Dear Dennis,

I am a 19 year old girl and I think that I have a venereal disease. I am very frightened, very lonely and very scared. Please help me. Could you please send me the name and address of a place that could help me? It must be a place where no punitive action will be taken, where my parents will not be told and where I can be both tested and treated. Please help me. . . .

Dennis,

Please quiet this problem. I have never been well educated in the area of sex. Can you get V.D. from manual stimulation of the sex organs? Papers say you can get V.D. from sexual contact, do they mean you only get it from going all the way or can you get it from what I have done? Just send me your answer as quickly as possible without letting my parents know. Please. . . .

Dear Dennis,

I have finally gotten the nerve to write to you about my problem. It seems to me that I have gotten syphilis within the last two months, or that is, I think so. My ignorance upon this subject has just baffled me. I've read a few books but they seem to avoid the basic subject. I wonder if you could tell me where a guy can go so that he could get some tests. Thanks for your help. . . .

Dear Dennis Benson,

Our whole family listens to you on Sunday evenings in the car when we are returning from Grandparent's home in Ohio.

We heard the boy calling in about "bad case of V.D." It got us talking (with our children 9 and 13 years old). This introduced the topic for our family discussion in a comfortable way.

It also brought up an incident in my life as a nurse. We had a patient—a fine, healthy, respectable 40 year old who was going blind, so he was in the hospital. He had had a very mild case of syphilis 20 years before. It was so mild he had no idea he had it until it was discovered as the cause of his blindness. It was so sad that I have always remembered it.

We concluded that it does point up the importance of waiting until marriage for sexual intercourse and if not this then at least get treatment early.

We like your program and like listening to it as a family. . . .

Dear Dennis,

I'm a 19 year old girl and for about 9 years I have been doing something that is so hard for me to explain. I just don't know how to write it. Every once in awhile I get this urge in me to get on our bathroom sink and sort of swing back and forth on my posterior end. I hope you know what I mean. I never have told anyone about it. I'm so scared to know *why* I do this. I'll try to explain a little more. . . .

Dear Dennis,

It was good to get your letter. You said I needed more outside activity. So I got a job which I have had since December. I have been going to dances and I belong to my youth group.

But for some reason I still do this terrible thing. This afternoon I did it and I couldn't stop. I got sort of scared because I don't know why I am doing this and have no one to talk to.

I was going to a dance tonight with my girl friend and some how I told her. She couldn't believe me. I said I needed someone to talk to. Then we got to the dance and she didn't do anything all night, no dancing or laughing. Later I asked her if what I told her bothered her. She said, "I don't know." She is my best friend. I know I shouldn't have told her but I couldn't stand it any longer.

Where can I go? I couldn't go to my pastor

because I don't think I could face him when I see him in church. Please help me!

Dear Dennis,

I quite by accident came across your program about two months ago. My reaction was favorable as I as a youngster had a very unhealthy environment.

Just a brief insight. I had one brother, two year older. He died when he was $8\frac{1}{2}$ years old. My father died when I was 11 and I have a mother who was possessive and one who permitted no social life.

In addition she remarried and it was hell on earth. I had no privacy and still don't. My mail is opened, my phone calls are screened or there is eavesdropping. I have had it rough if one would view it in the way today's young people do. But I lived through it. I would have been great if I had someone then who would have shown the injustice that was being done to me and guided me to a reasonable solution. This was not available to me. So, I can see where a program such as yours can serve a need.

Last Sunday I was a little taken back when you gave almost open approval of premarital sex when you questioned a woman who called about sexual behavior. You didn't stand up for the traditional morality but seemed to be challenging her to explain herself.

Often as a youngster one wanted to do things which he knew was wrong but he thought it best to refrain, to control his emotions or suffer the consequences, parent or teacher dis-approval or even ridicule by his peers.

Self-control is necessary in every walk of life, sex included. Youngsters know that this type of behavior is not proper or moral, even though they act as though they don't believe that.

You, in your position, must convey that love is

a beautiful friendship which is vital in life, but intimacies should be avoided until the consequences and commitments can be handled on a mature level.

Please help these youngsters as you do—30 years ago such help could have benefited me—but I pray you inspire them to have virtue also. God bless you!

Dear Dennis,

This morning as I was cleaning out a box of old things, I came across a letter from you dated exactly two years ago today. I'd written you about a problem I had about a guy I loved who wanted sexual intimacies, which I wasn't ready to give.

After re-reading your letter this morning, I felt I had to write you and let you know how things turned out. You told me that I . . . "should start reaching out . . ." to other guys. I remember how I felt the first time I read this. I was completely against it, as you can imagine. Also in talking about other guys, you said I should "just enjoy them for who they are, as persons." Well, it was very painful for me, but I eventually realized that you were right, and I consciously made my reach out.

There was one particular guy who was a great friend to me, Peter. Whenever I'd be in pain over this guy Sam, Peter would always be there and would comfort me.

Eventually I looked forward to being with him and we were the closest of friends with a beautiful relationship. This whole time, he knew what I was going through with Sam and now I know he felt all the pain I did. All this time a strong love built up between us—a true and genuine love.

After 8 months of knowing Peter, it dawned upon me that I did love him. It was such a brilliant revelation to myself. I just can't explain it. We both cried. We have been going together for a year and a half now and I'm truly happy. We have troubles now and then, that's normal. But I know that the strong foundation of love we have will carry us through.

Your advice to me to reach out was a real help in that I forced myself to do so. You affirmed my moral position and encouraged me to seek the kind of relationship which I sought. I knew it was the right thing to do.

Thank you so much for caring and reading my letters. I wanted to let you know that through your help I have found real love and happiness. . . .

Dear Denny,

I'm 17 and last August I was raped by two guys. It is a long story. I've been to two hearings and the trial has been postponed about three times.

Ever since the guys were arrested, I've been really upset and nervous waiting for the trail because I would have to tell everything that happened and I just want to forget about it.

I've talked to two lawyers and the D.A. and only one lawyer said I have a good chance of winning the case. The other two said I didn't at all and I would have to go through a lot of embarrassment for nothing. I decided a few weeks ago that I would have my dad drop the charges because I just can't go through with that trial.

I keep thinking that people where I loaf at think I'm just a pig, but I am not. I hope that this experience will not mess me up. I don't feel very good about myself anymore. . . .

There is no end to the flow of human need as it touches the realm of sexuality. Yet, with each phone call, each letter, one gets the impression that there is a rehearsal of major segments of life in concentrated form. The significant other becomes unshakable and open. Yet, it is vital that the foundation of his or her own sexuality be understood and explored.

10:26—A pregnant woman calls to talk about her marital crisis.

"Dennis?"

"Yes."

"I have this problem. I am married and I have a baby . . . and I am going to have another one . . . and it's not my husband's . . . it's my boyfriend's . . . I was wondering how I was going about to tell my husband. . . ."

"How do you think your husband is going to deal with this? I can imagine, but I am asking it anyway."

"He is going to . . . oh . . . kill me."

"How did this kind of thing happen? It is done and I am not judging you, but does this imply that you and your husband have had a bad relationship?"

"Before we got married my ex-boyfriend kept writing me. He was in the service. And he tried to break my husband and me up in the beginning. He told me to wait until he came home because —from Vietnam—and I told him I didn't love him and I didn't want no parts of him. I was up at my mom's and he came up to see me and my husband was working. He was talking and saying that he wanted to go out with me and that he still loved me and all that. I was scared and I didn't know what to do. At that time I still liked him a little bit. I didn't know, you know, who to go with. I didn't know if I should divorce my husband and go back with him or what. And that is how it all started."

"Wow. I don't know. How far along pregnant are you?"

"*Four months.*"

"You got to . . . deal with this soon. . . . There is no set pattern of how you tell your husband. I think that you have got to set up the context in which you can work through this and it's not going to be something destructive, in a figurative sense to all involved. Is there any kind of mediator or counselor whom you both trust? Someone who cares for you folks? I know that I played this role when I was a pastor in the church. This person can sit down with both of you and help you work this through the way that is best for you. Do you have someone like that?"

"*No. . . .*"

"Why don't you give me a call when I am off the air in about thirty minutes . . . and I will give you the name of someone who can help? There might be some violent emotion that may just get in the way of the issues behind this situation. If you folks can't sort this out, you will never be able to find some answers. You are obviously dealing with something very serious and I would urge you to give me a call after the show. Okay?"

"*Okay. Thank you so much. I'll call you.*"

There is a real sense of frustration as I listen to this woman. How can I be of help to her? There is no one answer to the problem she presents. I feel that she shouldn't have gotten herself into this position. However, that is really of no concern to us at this point. I felt like I was moving through a mine field as she talked. On reflection, my responses could have been almost funny. I asked things that should have been self-evident. Will she call back at 11:00? I do hope so. She needs counseling. This whole business of referral is so touchy.

Dear Dennis,
   I don't know if you remember me, I called you last Sunday and told you I was going to kill myself. You listened, asked me a couple questions and then told me to see a friend of yours. I called him Monday, told him my problem and then he asked a few questions. We decided it would be better to meet in person so we set up an appointment for Wednesday afternoon. I went in not knowing what to expect and went away not knowing how I felt. It was a question-answer session. He was trying to understand my motives. He went about it by trying to get me to analyze my feelings. He kept asking me how it felt inside. He told me he wanted to help me as much as he could and that he didn't want to cross the line of taking the choice away from me.
   He told me that I could call him whenever I felt especially bad or upset. I talked to him one other time on the phone because I felt really confused and upset. I don't find I can talk to him with ease, but we've only met once and he made me feel better. The biggest problem is that I feel that I have been pushed on from one person to the next. Now he thinks I should see another counselor. The trouble with this is that I don't want my parents to know. Your friend promised not to tell them. However, how can I trust this next counselor?
   I am supposed to see your friend tomorrow afternoon, but I can't help feeling that he's going to be frustrated and maybe even a bit confused. He's there trying to help me and I feel like I'm burdening him with my problem. What am I supposed to do? He's a nice guy. He seems to care and I will talk to him tomorrow, but I won't talk to anyone else.
   I am listening to the show now. You really seem to care and you are not afraid to admit it. I debated whether or not to call you. I wasn't sure

what would happen if I called you. I'm glad I
called and I'm glad you're on every week. . . .

As you sit in a studio rehearsing the role of a significant
other, you become painfully aware of the limitations im-
posed by the setting. In the heat of the broadcast encounter you must strain to hear and feel. The audio
rhythms of human concerns start to penetrate your whole
system. The slightest bit of falsification is amplified greatly.

The hardest moment in the encounter with a person who
really needs face to face counseling is the referral. I have
shared some of the ways by which we attempted to transfer our role to the next person in line. However, the task
of finding the right person is hard. Hanna's reluctance
about visiting with Paul is common. She is not really re-
jecting his help. She rightfully feels discomfort in having
to shift loyalties and trust. Her letter tells me that she
wants to affirm our contract. Hanna knows that our relationship must remain that of the significant other. Her
opening panic is that perhaps I am just getting rid of
her. My next letter will assure her that I care for her in
particular. This letter will also affirm her relationship with
Paul. He will stay with her in her problem. He can read
her signals about the additional referral. He may have to
work with the psychologist on her behalf with himself
talking the case over with the expert.

Yet, there are many times when counselors have called
and told me that my referrals have dropped out before
coming to the appointment. They will sometimes call and
then fail to show up. Casting out the electronic net to
enable people to get to the kinds of resources they need
cannot be expected to gather in everyone. It is interesting
that the people in our *Rap Around* community tend to
remain in relationship with me even when they won't follow
my referral suggestions. Perhaps there is so little demanded

to be part of our community that the risk is not much for anyone.

There is a degree of realism for those who accept the role of seeking to be significant to others. We know that we are not going to be the final agent of healing for the past, bestower of wisdom concerning the present, nor answer person for the future. Yet, the intersection of my life with another can be a turning point which will have important consequences for the present and future. This enables me to accept my limitations and failures. It also cushions—a little bit, anyway—the pain I feel for those who can't make that next step at this point.

One thing which makes my *Rap Around* experience so important for me is that it contains the dimension of follow-up to a degree that might be missing in some of the media models for helping. Yet, this is also tricky.

> Dear Dennis,
> I'm 15 and I'm glad to say that right now, I'm not writing to you because I have a "problem." I'm writing because I have some thoughts I'd like to express.
> I don't know if you ever realized how many tears and throbbing hearts you've healed with your miraculous help. You have a gift that no one else has. You have a way of putting things so clearly and nicely that even the way you talk cheers up a person. . . .
> There are lots of other people who are trying to do the same thing, but they don't really help. I wrote to this help column in the local paper a number of times, asking for help and do you know what kind of answers I got? I got a printed piece of paper, ¾ filled with publicity and "keep reading!" When I finally got to the answer to the question, I asked 3 or 4 months ago, it was only about two lines long and missed the whole idea

completely. I seriously believe that this columnist is doing no good at all. . . .

There is no place in the significant other's character cabinet to put down others who are attempting to help. My response to Sally is an explanation concerning the limitations these newspaper columnists have placed on them. They are published in many cities and can't possibly answer every letter personally. We are locked together in this helping community. We rejoice at each other's role and success.

Many of the letters coming to us are from folks who are under professional help. They often discuss the state of their relationship with their counselor. Since this is an important part of the therapy, I usually affirm the struggle they are facing and urge them to share these feelings with the person.

There are many people who simply can't find help. This seems like an amazing statement for those in an urban complex. We have agencies coming out of our ears. However, there is a wide gap between a person in need and those able to help.

Many reasons contribute to this situation. A certain amount of professional elitism mixed with a poor public image help contribute to the situation. A man may be a Doctor of Philosophy in English literature, but he still doesn't know where to go for his marital problem. This is heightened when you think of some of the people you have already met through *Rap Around*. Money is an imagined or real problem in many cases.

Dear Dennis,
I feel that I need professional, psychiatric counseling. I'm in a very deep depression and I'm not living the quality of life that I want to. Could you direct me to some people who might help?

I don't have much money so it will have to be either free or low-cost. I live in the south suburbs, but I could get to almost any place. . . .

Dear Dennis,

It began by my constant thinking—of many things. Sometimes I can't sleep because I just think too much . . . of people, of events, of myself. Now I am thinking that I may be a homosexual and what should I do? I am a 22 year old female, about to enter a teaching career. I have never participated in (I want to say "committed") any overt sexual act with another of my sex, but it's the subtle things I feel that bother me.

I am lonely, I want to be loved. But when I think of whom I would like to love me, it seems that these people are mostly other women.

Could you please advise me on this matter, I really need to talk to somebody, but who? As far as some type of counseling, I really can't afford much at the present time. . . .

Dear Brother Denny,

I've been having some super-big hassles. I have been a practicing homosexual for almost four years. I have been a born-again Christian (John 3:3) for five years. June 24 was the date of my conversion, and at the same time I had the mission "call." Satan let me go for a year before he started with me, but then, wow! He really got ahold of me. I am 20 years old now. I was 16 when a friend "brought me out." I was super-involved in the gay scene, yet here I was a Christian.

I have received a mission call to Korea during the last month. I love my Lord and I have given Him my life to do with as He wills. Homosexuality is wrong. I want to be 100% straight. Homosexuality is condemned by the Bible (Gen. 19 and Rom. 1). I have tried counseling, but could not afford it. Do I deny Christ and just give into the powers of Satan? Please, Denny, answer this as soon as possible. I need help *now* before I have a complete breakdown or become neurotic. I'm in a highly emotional state. This is why this letter (i.e. pleas) is so incoherent. . . .

10:30—Station Identification.
> **"This is KQV. Pittsburgh. I'm Dennis Benson. You are listening to *Rap Around*. This is an opportunity to share your ideas and feelings. Call us."**

A high school student calls in with a humorous comment. He is a regular caller.

"Growling Bear" is a local student who has a good sense of humor. He calls us with a two-minute routine every week. The series of puns are wheeled out in good fashion. The commentary tonight deals with his experience in school. He has actually received fan mail. This call acts as a break in the tension which can build up on the show. It has been a particularly "heavy night." Growling Bear accepted my invitation to visit me before the show one week. We had a good chance to talk. We are friends.

It is interesting to note that we simply don't receive many crank calls. It helps to have Pat talking to the folks as our phone producer. He raps with them a couple of minutes. Those who just want to make noises usually can't go to the depth of a conversation. However, I like to feel that our folks are returning the love we send out to them.

There are a number of people in our community who never call and don't seem to be stimulated by phone calls in their communication. One person who was important to us was originally a friend of Pat's. Josie was facing marriage. However, her heart condition demanded radical surgery. She went through a lot of pre-operative uncertainties. We spent some time on the show affirming her and asking for the *Rap Around* community to support her through prayers or whatever means of communicating hope for her well-being they chose. It was a very powerful gathering of the ranks around her. She came through the surgery in good style and is a striving, married, career person.

Occasionally we received unusual mail. Folks who have a very different perspective on life reach out to us. It is sometimes hard to experience those who have a radically different view of reality. However, the writing process is a good means of coming to grips with what these folks were trying to say. For instance, George picked me out for special help.

> Dear Dennis,
> If I am not president of ABC, disregard this letter completely and accept my apologies for making any statement that offends you. Please help me. I'm the man of the airways. Through an act of compassion there have been several references to me over the airways by songs and announcers that I was made president of ABC, but never had any written or verbal contact with the executives of your station.
> I guess that this must be because I am a shy person and have been afraid because I was afraid ABC would level charges. Lack of recognition, loneliness have made life pretty rough for me. I don't think I can wait till next spring for your station to help me when the TV series in over.
> I don't care about the money involved and royalties. I just want my dreams to come true. Please acknowledge to me first of all whether I am really president of ABC. If this is true, I would like very much for you to become one of my counselors when I am finally in public life. If you are

listening to the airwaves, you probably are aware of my problems.

My situation has made it almost impossible to live a normal life or get a regular job. I am not in financial trouble though. I am asking you to get in touch with the executives of the ABC international to convince them to help me now. I am terrified at many of the problems and I hope this letter doesn't put me in the hospital again.

Tell the executives that the season's TV trend is set and I'm certain that my decisions will result in most of the people listening the rest of the season. If this is not possible, please start the contact with the station that has been neglected by all. There must be something more than an unwritten agreement between me and ABC.

One time I met one of your disc jockies and the situation was so embarrassing and awkward that my image was damaged terribly. I don't want to meet any of them again.

Dennis, I could probably have a public life with gradual exposure. I don't want to work down at KQV or in any way associate with the disc jockies. I request all of this for the tremendous support I gave ABC. I thought it was an unwritten agreement that they would help me in other ways. I prefer a letter from you to a call, but then it might not reach me. . . .

There is a strange sense in which I seem to enjoy folks who have a nonlinear or illogical orientation. George has a sensible approach to his nonreal world.

One morning a neighbor knocked at our door. She asked if I would do her a favor. We were not acquaintances. Her son was in a local hospital. He had been picked up and committed to the psychiatric section. "You two seemed to get along well. I would appreciate it if you would visit him."

When I reached the hospital I already knew my friend's history. Jim had been a brilliant student at Midwest University. He was found wandering on the lake front without his clothes. He proclaimed to all that he was the savior. He escaped from the mental hospital and returned home. He had been in and out of several treatment centers. He has been diagnosed as being manic depressive.

The last time he had stopped by my home I was playing a Cat Stevens' LP. Jim sang new lyrics as he heard the music. His mind was so quick. He was acting as if he were two different people at once. One was on speed and the other was totally aware of reality.

He was sitting on the green couch in the recreation area of the hospital. Four or five patients sat around him in a drugged stupor. They just gazed out into space. Jim was talking and singing to himself. His eyes were widely engaging an invisible audience. As I sat down, he continued his rap by sweeping me right into it. It was a heavy theological trip. He was at one with the legions of the holy people who had lived, been created, or imagined by the whole human experience. He was filled with love as he worked and reworked the mystical ladder of holiness. While this conversation was going on, we also rapped about the present reality. He was distressed over the drug orientation of his doctors. They wanted to dope him into normalcy.

He had been picked up because he was simply wandering on a Sunday and calling out to all about the love of life. I told him that a fearful world was not ready for this kind of meandering love. In fact, someone, somewhere would hurt him for such outpourings. He sadly nodded. He knew that he could not go on the way he had. His sentences came in broken fragments with music and singing sandwiched in between the thought segments. We were comfortable. The vibes were flowing between us. I en-

163

joyed his company in this state more than I do most of the conversations at social gatherings. He felt so deeply about love. He cared about values and he knew exactly what the world is like. He knew what normalcy brings. We were bodily swaying and interacting in a strange, but authentic rhythm. He was my brother and we were at one with the universe. Our symbiotic communion was totally out of sync with this room of drugged patients. In fact, what we were sharing would be madness to most of the people outside of the hospital.

The crisis in the hospital was that Jim didn't want to take the medication which would stabilize him. This was the only way he could be accepted by society. When I got up to go, he said, "I love you. Not in a fag sense. I love you as a brother." We embraced and he kissed my cheek.

The next time Jim and I talked was when we happened to meet on the bus coming back from downtown. He had his hair cut and was wearing a dark suit and tie. The hospital treatment had been successful. He took his medication daily and could actually sit still and carry on a single-faceted conversation. He was tired and a bit down. He had been going from place to place in the quest of finding a job. It had been hard. It wasn't the rejections that distressed him. He could feel the kinds of conformity such tracking systems would demand. However, there were no arguments about the comparison between the normal life and his orgy of dreaming and thinking about love and freedom. He could now make it. It was just a matter of getting a job.

It is strange. I still love Jim. Yet, I felt more comfortable with him when he was considered mad. The vibrations were so close to the surface that you could actually get in rhythm and communicate very deeply. I have learned much about myself and what i am from people who are considered mad and mentally ill in our society. There is a bit of madness to the biblical prophets. There will always be externalized behavioral attributes which society calls madness when the struggle for honesty and idealism is being waged. Perhaps the significant other becomes a bit mad in the process of listening and caring. There certainly are moments when the rational and structured falls away and authentic human transaction takes place even when others can't recognize it.

10:33—A policeman calls to talk about the image of the profession and what young people should contribute to cooperation between the law and the public.

"Dennis, I am a policeman. I have a hard time making young people in our community understand that I am a human being too. For instance, the other night I stopped some teenagers and, of course, I had to arrest one for not having a license. They were a little bit perturbed because I was searching the car. We had to tow the car to the city garage. We do this not only to protect ourselves, but to protect the valuables of the individual. There are other things the young people don't understand."

"A lady called last week and complained about young people. What do you do with such calls?"

"When someone calls and complains, even when they don't give their names, someone from the force has to follow up on it. If the kids are on the steps of a church or building and someone complains we have to follow up on it."

"How do you feel when people in the community call policemen, pigs?"

"You can imagine. I get angry . . . no . . . it is

more than anger . . . it is sadness. I wish young people would go out and talk to police officers in general. It is when people don't know each other that they become animals and not humans. There are many officers who are not uptight with kids. They do want to communicate. I have eight kids. I care about them. I went out and fought with officials to get the kids to use the playground at midnight. We want the city to light up the basketball courts for the kids. Now we wouldn't take time out of our free time to talk to recreation leaders if we weren't concerned as policemen."

"Some people have called and claimed that there are policemen who use excessive force and don't seem to have the sensitivity you are talking about."

"There are also bad priests, bad teachers, and bad parents. This doesn't mean that we should give up on all the people in these jobs who are good. People get uptight because they see the uniform. There are a few bad officers. But I might not like a boy because of long hair. I know there are some bad young people with long hair. But I am willing to like him because he is a person. I might be against orange shirts, but I like him as a person. I do things that some young person might not like and he does things I don't like. This is the kind of world we live in."

"That's a beautiful philosophy. . . . How does the young person reach the police who have been excessive with him or her?"

"Just loosen up a little bit. Say to yourself first, 'What's my hangup with you. How can I get to you?' Go up and talk to the policeman. When you see him, wave to him. The thing that really gets the policeman uptight is that young people sometimes use their mouth to insult. The *policeman figures that you have to have respect for me first, then I can respect for you. If the young person could realize that the policeman is also an adult, things would be much better."*

"Good talking with you. Peace."

10:36—Girl calls to talk about the problems she is having in getting a boyfriend. How can she get a guy to like her? She is lonely.

Dear Dennis,

This may seem quite weird, but I don't even know why I am writing to you now. To find out something about myself that I don't already know? I don't know, because I don't even know myself. My life is just a great big merry-go-round of unreal dreams and wishes. But I do have myself convinced that not all of these are only fantasies. There has to be something left in this rat race world for me. I just don't know where it is. Who it is and why.

You are probably confused and wondering about all this so called dramatic talk. I think you're very kind and real. And to make it worse you have to listen to all that rubbish from those kids who just want to hear themselves talk. I will say that I hardly listen to your show anymore because I can't stand it any longer to sit and listen to all those kids with boyfriend or girlfriend problems.

It is so easy to live in peace to me, only I need the right atmosphere and setting. I am fourteen. I will tell you the truth, because no one has been convinced how old I have been for the last couple of years, since I look a lot older. But that is small petty talk which I hate. Though how can one hate? I am very strange, to myself, to people, to the world.

I have or let's say had, one *very* close friend.

We were bound together like glue and we promised each other life friendship together. We have the exact same mind track, and we really were close. She went on vacation last week and I did really begin to realize that there was something there that was going to pull us apart. Today she went and slept over at a girl's house without saying anything about it to me. I mean I have broken up with two friends on her account. Now I have none. I really don't care. I really don't. I know you'll say I shouldn't feel that way, but I honestly do. I love to live my own life alone.

My parents are separated, though they are living in the same house. My mother is a real estate salesperson and she works most of the time and goes out in the night. Both of them do. They both have someone else on the line, and they are very open about it. Don't say to talk to my parents or go to a counselor. It won't work.

So I am alone most of the day and my life is filled up with cleaning the house writing poems and watching TV. I am freaked out. Tonight when I heard that my girlfriend had slept over, I ran out of the house in my backyard and started rolling down the hill saying I'm on a rainbow. Now I am sane and I suppose when I'm in high spirits, I'll probably think of myself foolish for writing to you. Friends or family aren't my problem. Not one bit. I have been used and cheated on so many times that I have no feeling yet.

I love the ocean, fields, sun trees, the sky. I am a nature freak. There is a song on the Beatles, "Yellow Submarine" album called "Pepperland" an instrumental. I have actually closed my eyes and have been there, almost. I mean I don't know how anyone can use drugs. All I need is music. I could actually give you a full account of my visits there. I am sounding so immature and out of it now, I suppose, but I don't care. I have a good view of life too, I should remind you.

Now this part will sound so unreal you'll say, "What is this now?" The Beatles. They are my life. At least Paul is. I belong to the local fan club. For awhile there I kept dreaming unreal dreams about falling into his arms one day and used to devote my life to them as individuals. I mean it's a bad case. And in my visits to Pepperland, it's Paul who takes me away. It's always Paul who is there. But I have changed. It is foolish to devote my life to something as unreal as that. I feel I have gone too far. But I still love him and when I hear a sad love song or any for that matter, it's he who I think of.

I swear that if they ever get together and tour, I would go see them. I would be willing to run away in order to see them. What would it accomplish?

I did run away on Christmas morning this past year. It was morning and my mother was frying chicken. Our family has never and never will be any bit close since my mom and dad have constantly been arguing since I can remember. Well, I ran out of the house in pajamas and sock covered feet and just ran and ran up the street. It was freezing out. I ran to the woods about a half mile up the street. I sat there numb, singing. You see how strange I am? You probably don't want me condemning myself that way. Well, everyone was out searching for me, but they didn't find me. I came home on my own, numb as I ever was before. I mean I had to, I couldn't survive like that.

I did want to come home and when I did everything cooled off. Well, now I don't even know what kind of a problem it is, and it isn't any of these. I am just so mixed up. Yet, I feel I am going the right way. I love Hare Krishna. I feel I could be very deeply involved in it if I were allowed. I dislike church organization. It seems to me that they are not real. I know the Lord is the only answer in life. Do you know of any books that tell of Krishna and Indian religion methods?

Once I had been listening to "My Sweet Lord" in my living room and it appeared I saw him standing there in my living room. There were others behind him following Him, as if in a chant. But as these days have gone by my feelings don't seem as strong. I want to feel it again, but how? I have said about my friends that they don't matter to me because I feel I will find some other real people soon. My family isn't too bad I love them all, and even though the Beatles are and will always be a part of my life . . . forever, I realize I can't be childish about it.

I love Krishna religion and I want to get into it. I can visualize that everything is bound to work out someway. But tell me why am I writing this? You see, I don't know what is inside that is killing me. Something there, so hard to explain. I still dream, and write and resort to Pepperland or somewhere like an island. I know I always will. But I can see that I am changing more than ever, and there is so little to say in such a short letter. I am confused, I guess you will say in time I will find myself, and you'd be right but I just don't know. Maybe it is because I am depressed as of now. I don't know anymore. Here is a poem, why I am writing it don't ask me, I can't say. . . . This for you. . . .

10:39—A girl calls to discuss the feeling she has about the impending death of her mother. She has terminal cancer.

Dear Dennis,

A friend of mine just died last night. She was twelve. She was never one of my favorite people. But God knows she was human, and she lived and breathed and laughed and cried. And now she's dead.

I know that some person is smirking and thinking "it's good for her," or "at last." But she and all other people need love and how can one person hate another? Why Dennis, why? Right now my head's not together and can't think but I know I've gotta do something to make someone happy. And to let them know that someone cares. . . .

Dennis, I wish there were someway that I could meet with you and just rap about life and death. . . .

Dear Denise,

I'm listening to a kid talking about death on *Rap Around*. It's almost over. I liked it. I'm not afraid of death. I'm afraid of old age, of being a cripple, of being alone. I have set for myself certain goals that I want to reach, now I'm young and I look forward to my life. I'm afraid I will look back and find fault and get into the "if only." I don't want this. Now my life seems so great, I like it, will it last forever this way? I know it won't, everything changes and I want to accept it as it comes.

Dennis,

I'm 18 years old. My boyfriend, Harry, was killed in a car accident five weeks ago. I loved him very much. ALL of my friends are very kind to me, but they go about their own business and "avoid" mentioning Harry's name.

Diane, my best friend is the only one I can rap to about Harry. She used to double with us a lot. She misses him very much, too. It was a terrible experience. I have been taking pills to help me sleep at night.

To top this my dad and I haven't been getting along ever since I was 13. We love each other it's just that he has a very bad temper and beats me for little things like leaving a light on in my room. I want to *get away*. Diane and I are planning to go to either Denver or Chicago and work there.

My mother is against this. She thinks I'm trying

to run away from my problems. I need peace of mind!—I have to be free—to find myself again. When Harry died, a part of me died with him. . . .

Dear Dennis,

As I sit here with the tears streaming down my face, I will attempt to tell you what your show tonight has brought me.

A year ago Christmastime, I lost my only little sister. She was only 14 and had been sick for most of her life. I have no real friends and I loved Joanie as great as a sister could love a sister. For the last 4 years of her life, I bitterly wondered to its purpose. She lived with so much pain and suffering.

Now I know why. When Joanie died, I died too but I have been stimulated by a spark of life in me.

I know now that Joanie lived to teach me to love. She suffered to show me the value of life.

I am eternally grateful for what you've done to me tonight and always. . . .

Dear Dennis Benson,

I was listening to your broadcast when a young girl called in who feared that her mother was dying of cancer. I appreciate what you said to her.

I experienced a year of caring for my aged mother through terminal cancer following surgery. Your remarks to this girl could not have been more understanding of the situation. You felt she had indicated that she and her mother were not on the best of terms and that now this was of great concern to her. Your thoughts about how people living in the same house very often have problems even though they love each other deeply, were very helpful to me. You advised her not to dwell on this but to go on from here and be as kind to her mother as possible.

This all touched me very deeply, as it paralleled

my situation so closely. Through my mother's illness, we became very close and had a patience and understanding of each other which I shall never forget. All ill feeling vanished. (Most differences are usually petty.)

Though I regret her year of suffering more than I can possibly say, I shall always be thankful that we had this opportunity to express our love for each other (not in words so much as in deeds and in quiet ways) and that I was able to ease her way a little by caring for her to the best of my ability. As you said, holding her hand is a great means of communication and speaks volumes.

You could not have given this girl more understanding advice and I'm sure you comforted her. I do hope she was listening carefully.

I don't know what purpose this letter can serve, but I felt you should know that someone out here heard and was touched. . . .

The whole grieving and dying process has been warped by the media reenforcement of the worst aspects of the American cultural view of this part of life. Fortunately some great theological work is now being done concerning death and grief. On *Rap Around* people were often willing to share their encounter with death. People could emotionally hook into another person's experience. The significant other has a particularly useful role concerning this whole realm.

There were many times when we would become involved with a person as he or she would be related to the family unit. One member would write and soon another letter would come back from someone else in the house. This overlapping offered certain problems and opportunities. Certain confidences had to be maintained in spite of all the community among people involved in the communication process. The significant other is caught as being one who cares about the total family context of the person. It is so tempting to usurp the prior claim of other loved ones. We can easily become the hero and special person at the expense of parents or family. Yet, the main thrust of our relationships is to enable others to relate more fully to loved ones. These are real significant persons in the lives of others.

In one glut of communication four members of one family exchanged letters concerning their problems. The first person to write was a teenager (daughter). She had just run away and returned. Her mother added her side of the story. Over the course of three years I received letters from mother and daughter plus a serious boyfriend. The communication currently includes the youngest daughter in the family. The significant other can relate to warring members of the family unit because it is not a case of taking sides. We care for everyone in the family and their ability to relate to one another.

10:43—Girl calls to talk about the trouble she is having with her dad. He won't let her go to a dance with a guy she likes.

"I have a problem. I have been dating this guy who lives some distance away. He has asked me to the prom. I am afraid that my dad won't let me go."

"Has your dad met the guy?"

"Ya. He likes him."

"Have you talked to your parents about going?"

"I talked with my mom. She says that it is okay for me to go if my dad says yes."

"What kind of relationship do you have with your dad?"

"A distant one."

"Shame on you. (laughter). You should really have it together with your dad by this time. I am revealing my weakness, but your dad really needs you as a person. What kind of life does your dad live?"

"He works real hard. It is a job that is pretty dissatisfying. At least, he complains when he comes home. . . . He bowls and does things with my brothers. I am the only girl in the family."

"Let's suppose that you are a maturing woman . . . not just a child in the family. What are some of the things you could do that would be important to him personally?"

"Well, he sometimes complains that no one understands him or listens to his problems."

"What happens when he comes home from work?"

"Well . . . my mom and some of the others in the family usually rap with him about . . . things that happened during the day."

"What kinds of things?"

"Well . . . usually fights and things that (laughs) . . . I guess we kind of dump on him . . . it must be a hassle for him. . . ."

"It might be interesting to sit with him and ask him about his day. . . ."

"Ya . . . it certainly would be different. My mom doesn't even seem to do that. . . ."

"I suspect that as you get into your dad's head from the perspective of who he is and what he needs . . . he will come to discover you as a mature woman. . . . Those who can listen to others have a degree of maturity lacking in children. . . . I think that dads appreciate honest concern and attentions from their children . . . particularly."

"That sounds interesting . . . maybe I will give it some thought. . . ."

"Call me and let me know how this approach of love works in your relationship with your dad. Peace."

Dennis,

I'm all mixed up. My mom doesn't trust me cause my girlfriend (I'm a girl) has long hair and glasses, (not wire rims). My dad hates her and calls her a hippy . . . etc. and says he doesn't want her in the house.

She is no hippy (whatever that means) and she's very intelligent. She plays the piano and organ and has always been in the highest classes in school. They don't care. They still don't like her.

This affects me strongly cause she is so much like me. I'm too emotional and cry when my parents cut her down. It's as if they were disowning me. To make matters worse she has a boyfriend who has hair down to the collar of his shirt. Right now as I'm writing this my mom is sitting across from me and your program is on and she said, "What a weirdo!"

Please don't tell me to talk it over with my parents cause I have tried a lot of times and come away crying. . . .

Dennis,

I have a problem. My parents were divorced when I was 8. I am now 15 almost 16. My mom has remarried and my stepfather doesn't like me at all. When him and my mom have a fight, my mom takes it out on me and says I wasn't planned. In other words, she didn't mean to have me. She is always telling me to leave, but I have no place to go. I have a brother who is 17, but she seems to like him.

She always is yelling at me and gets mad when boys come to see me. Ever since I won the queen contest at our school dance she has been saying I'm no good, that I'm a flirt. No one else seems to think so and I don't try to be.

I'd like to leave and stay with a friend of mine. Their parents have agreed to adopt me legally, but my parents won't agree on anything with them. What should I do?

Dear Dennis,

I'm 15 years old. For the last 6 months I've been really thinking about *"running away."* I know that I'll probably be taking the "easy" way out, or hurting myself, but I don't know what else to do!

Ya see, I got a few E's on my report card and my parents grounded me for it. You know it can be a real hassle, especially in my house. All I do is sit around in my bedroom and it's a real drag and I don't think I can hack it anymore.

Ya see, Den, my parents are very cold people. It's real hard to talk to them. I can't even begin to try to talk to them.

Me and my father never could talk. I never was able to talk to him. We never got along. Maybe it's because I hate him. My mother and I used to be real close, but all of a sudden we seemed to drift apart and now we're always fighting.

I used to babysit for some lady on weekends, but my parents made me stop because they realized that I was pretty close with that lady. They did that to me all my life.

I know by running away it isn't going to prove anything, but I just have to get away. They've already told me to run away, because they would just put me away. I think I'll be a lot happier in a home. Ya see, my brother ran away 3 times and they didn't do anything to him. Instead of punishing him, they let him quit school and they bought him a new car just so he would stay home. Now he's king around the house. Everybody always has to do everything for him.

My parents said that they didn't know what to

do when my brother ran away, but they know what they'll do with me. They said they'll put me away, but I don't care. I guess that my problem is "not caring." Thanks for listening. . . .

Dennis Benson,

I am 13 years old and a boy. I really need help. My dad drinks pretty much. I think the reason he drinks is my mother. I am not trying to take sides here, because I think both are wrong.

I think my mother does make him do pretty much work. Once he does something like take her shopping she wants more. She'll ask him, after that, to fix something and this goes on and on. So to get away from her, he drinks and gets drunk. He comes home and starts swearing and calling her names.

I'm trying to help by going with him when he goes out. I talk to him. My mother thinks I only go with him to shoot pool and drink Cokes. I have tried to explain to her why I go, but we only get into fights.

To add to this hassle, my mother and dad have another problem. My 18 year old sister was planning to go into nursing, but now she can't. She can't because she changed her report card in chemistry from an E to a B. My mother also caught her smoking. A kid offered me a cigarette and I took it. I liked it, but I never started a habit because I think it is dumb.

I haven't missed one of your shows yet and I think it's really a help. I hope you get this letter soon and answer it soon. . . .

"Hello, Dennis, I'm 18 years old (male) and I'm going to college in town. It is a long way from my home.

"My problem is that I'm a homosexual and have a lover back home. He's about 26 and just recently I started this relationship between us, although I've known him since last year.

178

"I was heart broken to leave him back there for the first time after three other lovers—I really love him. I look up to him like he was my older brother.

"But since school is more important right now, how can I forget him? He means a lot to me and if he were to leave me, I'd kill myself! (I've tried suicide three times in my life so far.)

"The reason I love him is because he has filled a void that has been empty for a long time. My mother couldn't bring me up and all my parents did was buy me things. Dad usually let me have almost anything I wanted. Just this year my grandparents told me I was an accident. My parents really didn't want me as a person!

"I know homosexuality is supposedly wrong, but I won't change my ways. All I want to know is, how to forget about him until I go home again? If he doesn't feel the same about me as I do about him, what to do? The last time I lost someone I tried suicide and I almost succeeded. The next time I might really "leave this world." . . . Thanks for what help you can give me. Please hurry!"

This kind of call and the letters that follow in its wake are always so difficult. There are so many examples of cleavages between people who want love but cannot actualize it with those closest to them. It is painful to share in their lives (youth and adults) who believe that they are not loved by other members of the family unit. I assume that the feelings from the letters and phone calls are sometimes overstated. Perhaps reality is not what these folks perceive. Yet, if this is how one looks at reality, it must become a matter of serious concern.

10:45—Host comments on the letters received and urges listeners to write. He also thanks some listeners for sending down a box of cookies.

10:46—Girl calls to discuss a previous caller who spoke about the impending death of her mother.

Dear Mr. Benson,

I was reading Hamlet Sunday night and got interested in your show. I was particularly drawn to the caller who discussed her feelings in the light of her mother's probable death from cancer.

My niece just had an operation for a cistic hydroma. She is only one year old and I considered this very serious. Last week it returned and another operation was required. All my family was very upset. She is coming along well and it is a big relief. I do wish you could meet my niece.

This summer I spent with my sister and her husband and my other sister in one house. Everyday I would walk up the main campus with my niece on my back and meet my single sister. We would sit on the green and the baby seemed to attract kids. Kids who usually wouldn't give you the time of day would play with her. She is very open and warm baby and will always go to a friendly person. This showed me something. As kids grow older it seems they are not as open and I have noted this situation this year.

I am not one who prays conventional prayers, but I always try to talk to God. I hate to ask God for favors for myself because I feel selfish. I ask Him every night for peace—I wish that more than anything. I would now like to ask God for help and faith for the girl who called.

I feel that truth and faith and love are necessary for true peace. You and all others are in my prayers. . . .

10:48—Woman calls to discuss her consideration of divorce.

Dear Dennis,

I have a couple problems. I hope you can help me with them.

The first one is this. I am 23 years old. I have a 3 year old daughter. My husband is 35 years old. He told me when I met him that he was 27. We have been married for 2 years. Ever since we have been married he has lied to me. He never lets me go to work. I never had a door key. I have no phone. I have never been allowed to go anywhere without him or his mother.

He has not been home at night for over 3 weeks. He says he has a double job. I just see him about $1/2$ hour on Sundays. We have decided to get a divorce. The problem is this: how do I tell his mother? We live with her and by me not having any outside contacts, we have become very close. In fact, we are closer than my husband and me. I really love her and I don't want to hurt her.

Also, since this is her house, I'm afraid when she finds out, she'll put us out. I don't have anywhere else to go. But also, I hate to keep being her friend when I know it can't last.

Dennis, I need help. I'm so afraid and lost. What will I do without anywhere to go or turn?

10:52—Host makes some general comments about the show and closes.

"Wow! We were busy tonight . . . there were letters I didn't get to share with you. I will answer them this week. Some folks have written in a state of deep depression. . . . All we can say, brothers and sisters, is that we care. I know that there are a lot of you out there in our *Rap Around* community who are really lonely and confused . . . and very, very upset. You may be at your wits' end. . . . You are dealing with some very serious things. I guess that all we can say is: 'Don't give up. Don't despair!' I am saying that and I am not just walking away. Let me know. . . . I will get you in touch with some friends who are competent, caring people . . . who aren't going to rip you off . . . who aren't trying to use you. They are there to care for you. Sometimes you don't know where to find such people. That's one of the best things that *Rap Around* can do: to give you a glimmer of hope that it does help to talk to somebody who does care.

"*Rap Around* also affirms the fact that you can go on to find someone to work through the problem with . . . so, drop me a note. Our community embraces all kinds of people. There are folks of all ages. I get letters from people 70 years old. I get letters from homosexuals, from lesbians, people who are lonely, people who are frightened and people who are very happy . . . and we do love all of you and we do care about you. We are trying to be here . . . to be . . . brothers and sisters. So if you drop me a note, I will answer and try to help you make the kinds of decisions that you have to make about your life. Okay? Thank you engineer, John Yurek. Thank you, brothers and sisters. Peace and power . . . (music from theme).

6 Coming Down

I gather up the papers with one scoop and head for the door. Lynn and Carolyn will take over immediately after the news with their talk show. Pat has a bunch of calls lined up for me to take off the air. The first call is from the woman who called during the show. She promises to visit the counselor on my suggestion in order to work on the problem with her husband. Several other calls follow in rapid order. Two calls are from parents who wanted help in relating to their children. A partially blind girl calls to seek help about the problem she and her blind roommate are having getting an apartment. They are being hassled by red tape.

Pat and I spend a couple minutes debriefing the show and the thrust of the calls. After signing out and bidding Russ good-night, it is the parking lot and home. It takes several hours before the *Rap Around* experience has settled into the back of my mind, and I can relax. It has been an exciting and moving night. My head swims with people.

You have met a lot of our people in the course of reliving an evening in the life of *Rap Around*. I hope that you have also discovered the beauty and possibility for a more complete humanity through the sharing and caring suggested by these folks. I have let them speak, cry, and rejoice. Perhaps it has been suggested that the real answers to the problems they raise must come from the people themselves. Their words, thoughts, and feelings are the pure poetry of the struggle for authentic and full existence. I love these people.

The two hours of *Rap Around* that you have experienced was a reconstruction. This had to be. The show no longer exists. It was a very successful show, but was a victim of the station's attempt to win a different audience. Radio stations in major market areas make frequent shifts in target audience to please future advertisers or just keep alive in the face of strong shifting competition. At one point, the ratings suggested that 72% of the teens in our area were listening to the show. We were presented The Golden Mike Award as Pennsylvania's best local radio program in the interest of youth. The honor was bestowed upon us by The American Legion Auxiliary. A bishop, an air force general, and numerous other folks stopped me at one time or another in the street or air terminal and commented about listening to the show.

Pat and I were saddened by the demise of the show. However, this is an excellent reminder that the significant other's role is not dependent on any particular setting or occasion. This kind of transaction unfolds in any context. There simply needs to be two people. *Rap Around*'s demise also suggests that our kind of communication does not have longevity. People stop and interact. However, they will soon move on to other, and hopefully, more complete relationships with others.

The caring stranger, volunteer in a hospital, nursing home, or meals-on-wheels program knows all of this. It may sound like the Lone Ranger syndrome ("Who was that masked man?"). However, this nurturing love is the foundation for so much potentiality for other people. It is

184

a vital work that only a person such as yourself can undertake.

The significant other is a style of caring which returns so much more than you can ever give out. In the course of exchanges with people you become acutely aware of your own limitations and needs. However, much healing and strength simply come as you reach out and care for others. The persons who trust you and turn to you affirm your own authenticity. They give you wholeness which is missing from self-directed, non-embracing life.

This book is not really about a radio program. The fact that it took place in Pittsburgh or that I was the host is not very vital to the premise offered here. This story is a witness to a style of caring that is needed and possible even in the most casual relationship. Any age person in any setting can undertake our kind of communication. Within each person there is some discerned need for a significant other at some point.

Fortunately there is a whole new breed of people who want to reach out and touch others. They are in churches, youth groups, community clubs, service groups, or just by themselves. It is to this new race of caring people that the mantle of being significant to others is passed. The hopes and dreams of becoming a community rest in this low profile of care and nurture. I hope that you have been encouraged to continue this work or perhaps undertake it for the first time. This is a rich kind of existence.

7 Closing Credits

Rap Around was a community. Dear folks made it live. You have heard their inner voices in this book. Their lives have been so that we all might be more complete. This book has been of them, by them, and for them. I thank them for giving us wisdom, sensitivity, and hope through the witness of their pain and joy.

Brother Patrick Carney is a creative and loving teacher who made our wired community work particularly well. He was the first line of greeting when our radio folk called. It was his care and understanding which helped callers translate their humanity into our public conversation.

Russell Martz—the watchman—John Yurek, Bob Harper, Mary Haynes, all my KQV colleagues, Betsey McClure—my ace secretary—and countless others made the practicalities of our experience possible through the gifts of their technical skills and their open commitment to our kind of community. David H. Barnes once again helped to weed out errors in the typed manuscript.

Most of all my family has snuggled me in an environment which permitted me to reach others. Marilyn, Amy, and Jill have loved and understood when piles of letters had to be answered. Sometimes this has meant that some of their priorities had to be shelved while we made that call or visited that person who particularly needed a significant other.

The *Rap Around* folk opened my eyes and heart to a new world of care and hope. This community was a stop on a hard road. We were strangely warmed and comforted before facing the trials before all of us. We were all better for attempting to be significant to others. May God bless all of us. May our quest offer a challenge and a possibility for you.